D0563064

THE SCHOOL OF HARD TALKS

MAY 1 6 2023

Hampshire County Public Library
153 West Main Street
Romney, WV 26757

HOOL ^OF TALKS

HOW TO HAVE REAL CONVERSATIONS WITH YOUR (ALMOST GROWN) KIDS

EMILY KLINE, PhD

SASQUATCH BOOKS
SEATTLE

Copyright © 2023 by Emily Kline

All rights reserved. No portion of this book may be reproduced or utilized in any form, or by any electronic, mechanical, or other means, without the prior written permission of the publisher.

Disclaimer: The Publisher makes no representations or warranties with respect to the accuracy or completeness of this work, and specifically disclaims all warranties, including without limitation warranties of fitness for a particular purpose. No warranty may be created or extended by sales or promotional materials. The advice and strategies contained herein may not be suitable for every situation. This work is sold with the understanding that the Publisher is not engaged in rendering medical, legal, or other professional advice or services. If professional assistance is required, the services of a competent professional person should be sought. The Publisher shall not be liable for damages resulting herefrom. The fact that an individual, organization, or website is referred to in this work as a citation and/or potential source of further information does not mean that the Publisher endorses the information the individual, organization or website may provide or recommendations they/it may make. Readers should be aware that websites listed in this book may have changed between when the work was written and when it is read.

Printed in the United States of America

SASQUATCH BOOKS with colophon is a registered trademark of Penguin Random House LLC

27 26 25 24 23   9 8 7 6 5 4 3 2 1

Editor: Sharyn Rosart
Production editor: Rachelle Longé McGhee
Designer: Tony Ong

Library of Congress Cataloging-in-Publication Data
Names: Kline, Emily (Clinical psychologist), author.
Title: The school of hard talks : how to have real conversations with your
    (almost grown) kids / Emily Kline, PhD.
Description: Seattle : Sasquatch Books, [2023] | Includes bibliographical
    references and index.
Identifiers: LCCN 2022038686 | ISBN 9781632174703 (paperback)
Subjects: LCSH: Children and adults. | Teenagers–Family relationships. |
    Interpersonal relations. | Motivation (Psychology)
Classification: LCC BF723.A33 K55 2023 | DDC 155.5–dc23/eng/20221017
LC record available at https://lccn.loc.gov/2022038686

ISBN: 978-1-63217-470-3

Sasquatch Books
1325 Fourth Avenue, Suite 1025
Seattle, WA 98101
SasquatchBooks.com

For Dale and Greta, the brightest stars in my sky

CONTENTS

CHAPTER 1

WHAT IS A PARENT'S JOB?

To get to know a new family, I sometimes ask the parents to take a moment to imagine a scene in the life of their family ten years from today. What do they see? Who is present? Where are they? What is the topic of conversation? I encourage them to envision a best-case scenario.

Parents conjure scenes of Sunday night dinners, afternoons on the beach, meeting eventual romantic partners, or reuniting for holiday celebrations. They see themselves bantering happily about jobs, friends, books, food, or current events. The mood in these scenes is light; there is no agenda other than spending time together as a family.

Imagining children as adults can be a helpful way to take a mental break from the exhausting work of getting an adolescent to complete homework or hang up a towel in the proper spot. The exercise helps parents to refocus on the bigger picture, in which their relationship with their child is the most important goal. I've never heard a parent say, "I imagined telling my twenty-five-year-old to take a shower, he went and did it, and then he put his towel on the hook in the bathroom without a reminder." Instead, they are excited to see their child as independent and interesting, someone with whom they can relax and have fun. The weight of responsibility for the daily grind of chores, school, and acceptable behavior is lifted, and they can appreciate their child as a person. Most important, they experience a flash of curiosity about this adult they've never met: What might he look like? What will he say?

I also ask parents to tell me about their own adolescence; specifically, how they related to the adults in their lives as they were coming of age. The answers tend to be complex. Except in extreme cases, their memories of their own parents aren't good or bad— instead, most of us recall our parents as *people* who loved their children and raised them in ways that were informed by a mixture of culture, personality, and circumstance.

Reflecting on their own upbringing, parents talk about the adults in their world with whom they could be themselves. These were the mentors they sought out to discuss their dilemmas. These might have been small issues: what to wear to a birthday party, where to sit at lunch, soccer versus basketball. Parents recall that they confided most in adults who listened, withheld judgment, and allowed them to make up their own minds about how to navigate their world. These qualities demonstrated the adults' sincere interest in their inner lives and set the stage for good conversations.

Sometimes these adults were parents, but often not. Parents' intense feelings of responsibility for the safety and future of their children can interfere with listening. A family friend, neighbor, or grandparent who doesn't carry that weight might have the ability to truly hear what the child is saying without any particular anxiety about how the situation might resolve. Hypothetically, whether a sixth grader plays soccer or basketball after school seems inconsequential. Yet with your own children, feelings inevitably arise. You know too much: your oldest daughter chose soccer, and the coach was terrible, and she dropped out midway through the season. We feel compelled to share this information. There is nothing wrong with this instinct, yet it interferes with kids' ability to take stock of their own world. Suddenly the dilemma is no longer about soccer versus basketball but, rather, whether to heed their parent's advice.

When You Listen, They Listen

Parents are under pressure. It comes from school deadlines, the competitiveness of social media, and the judgments of extended family, but mostly it comes from within. Many of us have internalized to some extent the idea that our children are an extension of our*selves.* When our kids struggle, we feel the shame of having somehow failed. When they succeed, we bask in their glory, confident we must have done something right.

In this book, I'm going to challenge that view. Parents cannot control how their kids turn out. Whether kids wind up earning a lot of money, developing depression, or summitting Mount Everest doesn't reflect much on the competence of their caregivers. Expectations about how they should dress and talk; whether we push them toward advanced classes or after-school jobs; whether we allow them to go out with friends on school nights or attend parties—your opinion about these issues matters mostly to the extent that your adolescent cares what you think. Therefore, the most important work of parenting an adolescent is not controlling your child's path, but rather creating a relationship of trust and mutual respect.

Parents, particularly by the time their children reach adolescence, have far less influence than they may imagine. Just think about how siblings raised in the same household can turn out to have such different personalities and lifestyles. To a humbling extent, children barrel through this world with much of their programming in place. Once basic needs for sustenance, safety, and belonging are met, the impact of household ethos is mostly eclipsed by the more powerful forces of genes, peers, and culture. Even in infancy and early childhood, kids have preferences and personalities that actively filter and shape the world around them. By middle school, they are quite independent. Not in terms of being able to care for themselves and meet their own needs, but in the sense that they inhabit a fully realized social and psychological world that is mostly separate from their parents.

Yet anyone who has recently interacted with a twelve-year-old (or, ahem, a college student) recognizes that they are far from ready to take responsibility for major decisions. The prefrontal cortex, the part of the brain responsible for planning, risk estimation, and self-awareness, continues to develop through about age twenty-five. Studies show that relative to adults, adolescents tend to downplay risks, react more impulsively, and suspend their better judgment in the presence of peers. Although young people desire and benefit from a measure of autonomy, they are much better off if there are trusted adults in their lives who can steer them away from a poorly considered tattoo, credit card, or romantic entanglement.

Adolescence and early adulthood are also a time of heightened risk for mental health problems. Young adults ages eighteen to twenty-five have the highest prevalence of mental illness of any age group, and suicide is the fourth leading cause of death globally for adolescents. Even before the COVID-19 pandemic, 29 percent of people in this age group met the criteria for a diagnosis according to the Substance Abuse and Mental Health Services Administration. The emotional impact of COVID restrictions hit young people particularly hard. In the United Kingdom, the number of teens who described themselves as having poor mental health increased 60 percent over the course of 2020. In the United States, surveys found that nearly half of parents of teens and

95 percent of college students felt that the pandemic had negatively impacted their mental health. School social workers, college counseling centers, child psychiatrists, and emergency rooms were overwhelmed by the surging treatment demand from young people with mental health problems. In this context, promoting self-sufficiency may seem riskier than keeping a close watch.

What, then, is a parent's job? Parents of adolescents must prepare their children to function independently while remaining close by to provide logistical support and—if all goes well—to offer comfort and guidance when needed. This is easier said than done. Teens are notoriously uninterested in heeding adults' limits and advice, setting the stage for years of conflict. Insisting on control over adolescents' behavior drains warmth and authenticity from the relationship, and they will often find a way to circumvent parents' rules, or simply withdraw emotionally.

If parents hope to influence adolescents' decisions and monitor their safety, they need to find a way to be present, close, credible advisors—in short, the kind of people whose advice kids might actually want to hear. Don't worry: I want your child to hear (and follow!) your advice. This book offers a vision of how to achieve that goal as well as guidance on simple, specific communication strategies that you can use to build a new kind of relationship with your child. The guiding principles are recognition of your child's personhood and inner world, curiosity about their experiences, and optimism about the possibility of meaningful conversation and mutual understanding. The more genuine your interest in the person your child is becoming, the more influence you will wield as they embark on that process. Put simply: when you listen, they listen.

Adolescents seek out adults who demonstrate interest in their ideas and dilemmas, express confidence in their abilities, and encourage them to solve their own problems. By working closely with hundreds of parents, I have developed concrete and reproduceable methods for accomplishing those micro-tasks. I don't use scripts; instead, I teach simple conversational tools and a five-step "guide" to hard talks that can be deployed to discuss any topic.

A brief note on terminology: in this book I will use an expansive definition of *adolescence* as the developmental stage that starts with puberty and ends when adult roles and relationships are fully established, a period that in much of the world corresponds roughly with ages twelve to twenty-five. Thinking of youths in their early twenties as adolescents might strike some readers as odd, but it's a useful shorthand. Similarly, I am going to default to the term *parent*, although I am hopeful that this book will also be helpful to all kinds of caregivers, including grandparents, stepparents, foster parents, educators, and other adults who are deeply invested in the lives of young people. For readers curious about the studies and books that inform my writing, there is a list of references organized by chapter at the end of the book.

What Is the School of Hard Talks?

I am a practicing psychologist (I treat patients in a clinic), a clinical supervisor (I teach students how to do psychotherapy), and an academic researcher (I conduct observational studies and clinical trials). The goal is that by balancing these roles, I can integrate the continuous feedback I receive from my patients, students, and research data to ascertain what truly works best for families.

This book presents my observations from several years of research into the communications of parents and their adolescent children, as well as two clinical trials in which my colleagues and I created a "school of hard talks." Parents who enrolled in the "school" (i.e., one of our research studies) received either group or individual coaching to learn a communication technique called motivational interviewing, while my research team tracked and analyzed the impact of this coaching on their communication habits, mental health, attitude toward their parenting role, and relationships with their children. Parents who participated in these trials described their kids as struggling with the full range of teen and young adult problems—from academic difficulties to loneliness to marijuana use to suicidal thinking. They came from many walks of life, as you will see in the case descriptions, which are loosely based on real people. This book is not about my own experiences as a mother—though I am one, which I think strengthens both my empathy and insight into my patients' challenges.

The results of my research are preliminary but compelling enough that I feel no ethical qualms about recommending these strategies. After learning the techniques outlined over the following chapters, parents felt significantly less stressed and more confident. They also reported less family conflict and less personal resentment and burnout about their caregiving role. Parents identified changes in their communication style, increased self-awareness, better relationships, and better mental health—both their own and their child's. Here are quotes from a few parents who participated in either individual or group coaching in response to the question "What's changed?"

> I've become a much better listener and am able to show understanding and support without engaging in a disagreement.

> The children are willing to listen to me, not just dismiss what I am saying.

> I find that I hold back on criticizing my child for her decisions and instead I try to find out from her what her motivations are by asking curious questions rather than judging.

> I think I have more productive discussions with my children and that makes me feel better about myself and as a parent.

> My daughter feels validated and heard, which has decreased her acting out and outbursts.

I've spent most of my career researching and treating serious mental illness, and my original idea was to teach this communication approach to caregivers of young adults dealing with psychotic disorders like schizophrenia. I constantly used motivational interviewing when interacting with my own patients, and I found myself wanting to offer more in-depth coaching in these concepts and strategies to the parents of the young people I saw in clinic. Over time, however, I realized that anyone could benefit from learning these tools.

In one of my studies, seventy caregivers whose child, grandchild, or sibling was suffering from psychosis met with me or a therapist on my team to receive coaching in the "hard talks" approach. Nearly all the study participants reacted with a curious mix of relief and frustration as they learned and practiced the skills. Relief because they experienced immediate benefit from trying the technique at home; frustration because they had been through so much and were only now learning effective communication strategies. I lost count of how many times I heard someone say, "Why didn't anyone tell me this ten years ago?" or, more sadly, "I just don't understand why my family had to go through this crisis before we could learn how to talk to each other." So, it is at the passionate urging of these families that I am writing this book for all parents.

Expressed Emotion

I came to this area of study through my two clinical interests: adolescent development (which is universal) and psychosis (which is unusual). Because psychotic disorders such as schizophrenia and bipolar disorder do not usually emerge until around age twenty, these interests have sometimes competed with one another for time and usefulness. I was lucky to find mentors and colleagues in a research community dedicated to developmental psychopathology, or the study of how mental disorders develop, what early symptoms look like, and how treatment or public health interventions might prevent some manifestations of serious mental illness.

It was through this research process that I became interested in a concept first described in the 1950s but somewhat neglected in psychological circles today called expressed emotion. As defined in the research literature, expressed emotion has facets that are both negative (hostility, overinvolvement, and criticism) and positive (encouragement and warmth), which can be observed in how parents talk about their children and their caregiving role.

A plethora of studies showed that schizophrenia patients whose parents voiced a lot of the negative aspects of expressed emotion were more likely to have a recurrence of symptoms and needed to return to a hospital for more treatment. Subsequent research showed that expressed emotion was not specific to schizophrenia at all. Caregivers' negative expressed emotion, especially their critical comments and overinvolvement, were found to predict severity and chronicity across a wide range of illnesses experienced by adolescents and young adults. This includes both psychiatric problems like anxiety, depression, and eating disorders and also, fascinatingly, medical issues such as juvenile diabetes and kidney disease. In a 2015 article, UCLA researchers described expressed emotion as "one of the most robust predictors of long-term outcome in the adult psychopathology literature."

Well that really excited me! This seemed like actionable information: if I could find a way to lower negative expressed emotion among the families I saw in clinic, and replicate that method in a research protocol, then I might really be able to help families avoid the most feared outcomes of chronic, serious mental illness. This theory also has the benefit of being intuitively easy to understand. Parents who feel perpetually annoyed by their kids, do too many things for them, yet still worry about their health and safety all the time get burnt out. And try as they might to keep that burnout private, it shows up in interactions and impacts the mood of the whole family.

It's important to clarify that parents cannot cause psychiatric or medical problems by being overinvolved or occasionally expressing a critical attitude. There is just no serious research that supports this theory. Unfortunately, the concept of expressed emotion became associated with harmful beliefs that parents are to blame for their children's mental illness, which psychiatrists and psychologists accepted and perpetuated for years. In a classic instance of throwing the baby out with the bathwater, interest in expressed emotion faded over time. Some senior researchers told me directly that studying expressed emotion was anti-parent and intellectually passé.

Despite these warnings, I began to examine expressed emotion in the families of adolescents seeking treatment for a diverse array of problems, from academic setbacks to serious mental illness. I found that in these samples, expressed emotion wasn't particularly associated with demographic factors like income or race, nor was it reliably higher among parents of adolescents with any particular diagnosis. But overall, parents who agreed with statements indicating negative expressed emotion toward their children (for example, *I'm so worried about them; they annoy me; I've given up too much for them; they don't appreciate me*) also reported that they were highly stressed, lacked confidence in their parenting, and had a lot of conflict with their children. This type of statistical correlation tells us that these factors—expressed emotion, stress, low confidence, and conflict—are closely related to one another, but it doesn't give any clues about the underlying cause. But it was clear that expressed emotion was not just an abstract concept with prognostic meaning to researchers; for the caregivers in my studies, it was strongly associated with stress, fighting, and feeling like they had no idea what they were doing.

Of course, expressed emotion is far from the only or even primary environmental influence that can impact child and adolescent psychological development. Kids who face true adversity—such as having parents who struggle with addiction, witnessing community or domestic violence, or experiencing physical or sexual abuse—often suffer lasting wounds. Throughout their development, all children need physical and psychological safety in the form of reliable caregivers, safe places to sleep and learn, predictable routines, and a sense of welcome and belonging in their community. If parents or the community at large cannot meet those needs, then children's psychological development may be adversely impacted, resulting in dysregulated stress hormones, difficulty trusting others, and exaggerated sensitivity to physical and social threats—some of the building blocks of mental illness.

But unlike the clear causal association between serious childhood adversity and later mental and physical health problems, the link between parents' expressed emotion and kids' mental illness is much more nuanced—and in my interpretation, hopeful. Other than in extreme circumstances, parents do not create their kids' mental health problems. But they are also not helpless in the face of their adolescents' suffering. Caused by an interaction of inherited vulnerability and environmental stress, mental health issues can creep up in any family. But parents who are well-equipped can make a huge difference in helping vulnerable adolescents to avoid despair or get back on track after a derailment.

What does it mean to be well-equipped? In my mind, the equipment is a relationship that is warm and supportive, the ability to communicate openly, and the fortitude to weather inevitable conflict with some grace. Parents don't have to be perfect. They don't need to read long books about adolescent development or become experts on substance use, mental health, or college admissions. They don't have to be Zen masters who never show irritation. They don't need to communicate in a specific way or say/not say certain things. If a family has a style that works for them, who cares if it complies with what some psychologist recommends?

For many parents, though, open communication and a generally warm relationship feel pretty far off. In general the parents I see in my clinic and research studies are kind, caring, and fun to talk with—in short, "normal." But they struggle mightily to communicate with their adolescents, and they are highly motivated to find new and more effective ways to relate. Their experience of being unsure how to approach important topics with their kids is not unusual. A 2018 survey found that the vast majority of parents admitted they "struggle to communicate meaningfully" with their kids, that their kids "avoid talking to them if they don't have to," and that they sometimes feel "shut out of their child's life."

So, if you are part of this tongue-tied majority, you are not alone. This book is for you. Over the next few chapters I will lay out a philosophy and a practical guide for establishing closer and more respectful relationships with the adolescents in your life. The concepts and skills represent an approach called motivational interviewing, which is a style of communication widely used by therapists to help their clients adopt healthy behavioral changes such as reducing drug use, taking medications as prescribed, or getting to the gym more often. Please approach it with a spirit of experimentation: read on, try anything that appeals to you, and observe the effect on your children, relationships, and family life. Decide for yourself what works for your family.

Although many of the parents who participated in my research did the "school of hard talks" on their own, others did the training with their spouse or logged on to Zoom in small groups to learn, discuss, and practice skills. Parents who worked through the concepts in community with others seemed to especially benefit, because in addition to learning the skills, they wound up feeling less alone with their challenges. Notably, some women who did the training on their own reported that even though they felt it helped them tremendously, they were then frustrated by the work of trying to explain their new approach to a skeptical co-parent. Consider reading, discussing (maybe debating), and practicing the ideas and skills in this book with your partner, friend, book club, or religious community—you will get more out of it.

Hard Talk Highlights

- The most important work of parenting an adolescent is not controlling your child's path, but rather creating a relationship of trust and mutual respect.

- If parents hope to influence adolescents' decisions and monitor their safety, they need to find a way to be present, close, credible advisors—in short, the kind of people whose advice kids might actually want to hear.

- Adolescents seek out adults who demonstrate interest in their ideas and dilemmas, express confidence in their abilities, and encourage them to solve their own problems. Put simply: when you listen, they listen.

- Mental health issues can creep up in any family. Parents who are well-equipped can make a huge difference in helping vulnerable adolescents to avoid despair or get back on track.

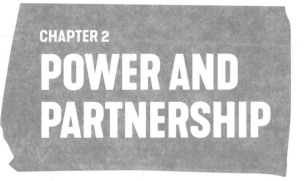

CHAPTER 2
POWER AND PARTNERSHIP

One stock phrase you often find in the parenting teens literature is this: "You can't be your child's best friend." And to that I reply: don't worry, you're not!

In all seriousness, many parents fear that they could diminish their authority by suspending judgment, even momentarily, when kids confront them with questionable decisions or broken rules. They feel that they have a duty to warn or to challenge when teens state an opinion that seems ill-informed. Or they worry that they need to choose between acting as a stern defender of rules and being permissive or indulgent.

This binary—permissive versus controlling—is both unhelpful and untrue. It is possible to be both understanding and authoritative. For parents who feel that consequences are an important tool, I want to reassure you that it is possible to use both curiosity (*Tell me more about your night—what kept you out past curfew?*) and consequences (*Well, I guess we both know this means* [insert consequence here]), so long as you sequence those correctly.

For parents who have more or less given up on imposing these types of consequences due to the warfare they tend to incite in your household: I see you, I know you, and I don't think that you are falling down on the job. Many parents have told me that grounding kids or limiting their access to electronic devices— essentially using isolation from friends as a punishment for rule breaking—has backfired so spectacularly that they have taken these strategies off the table completely. Others have noted that confiscating their child's phone specifically has caused a usually mild-mannered teen to react with unexpected aggression. These parents usually feel a great deal of shame; they judge themselves as weak and helpless in the face of their child's rule breaking or defiance. They feel they have failed to live up to the basic expectation of not being merely their child's friend.

You can't be a friend: Where did that specific admonishment come from? In the 1960s, psychologist Diana Baumrind defined two aspects of parents' behavior that created a useful way to think about parent-child relationships. These are responsiveness (the degree to which parents address children's needs in a warm and supportive way) and demandingness (the extent to which parents expect children to comply with household rules). Baumrind theorized that the ideal parent was both highly responsive and highly demanding, a style she defined as *authoritative*. According to Baumrind, authoritative parents communicated consistent rules and boundaries, as opposed to *authoritarian* parents who expected total obedience, and permissive parents who acted more like—here it comes—their child's friend. Our cultural consensus about not being your child's friend probably stems from her legacy.

However, this theory was formulated to describe parents' interactions with preschoolers, not adolescents. Baumrind also studied parent-adolescent interactions at a time when most of her contemporaries believed that teens and young adults should be independent and that efforts to control or shape their behavior were misguided or even harmful. Baumrind disagreed. She thoughtfully described a process of encouraging adolescents' individuality while remaining emotionally connected, and she found that adolescents whose parents communicated warmly and openly about household expectations were more socially responsible and less likely to use substances than those whose parents were more detached. Rather than pitting the concepts of independence and connectedness against one another, she argued that adolescents could become autonomous while remaining close to their parents and other adults in their communities. "Who persons are and will become," she wrote, "is defined by the communities they inhabit and the activities in which they engage. From this perspective, attachment to family and community facilitates individual development at any stage."

It's important to remember that until recently, kids were expected to grow up fast. In the 1970s typical twenty-one-year-olds in countries such as the United States and Canada were already married, working, and settled into long-term roles. Teens functioned more or less independently, and adulthood truly began at the end of high school. Over the past hundred years, our culture has radically changed in how we think about and treat teens and young adults. Today it is considered normal for young people to delay full-time employment, parenthood, and financial independence through their mid-twenties. In wealthy nations, children from well-off families are usually the last among their peers to hit these milestones of independence, which suggests that delaying adult responsibilities offers some advantages in our current cultural and economic context. Amid this role upheaval, parents may be unsure where they stand. Are adolescents essentially children who should follow parents' rules and face consequences for defiance? Or should they be treated more like adults who are financially dependent but intellectually and socially mature?

From my observations of parent-adolescent interactions, I have developed my own elaboration on Baumrind's model. In any given situation, I consider the degree to which parents can encourage independence (as opposed to trying to control or stay involved with every decision or behavior), as well as the extent to which they can accept their child's identity and preferences (as opposed to criticizing them). A parent who is highly accepting but overinvolved is the so-called helicopter parent, always hovering to ensure a preferred outcome. A parent who expects self-reliance and criticizes their child's identity and preferences might be considered rejecting. A parent who is both critical and overinvolved fits the expressed emotion profile described in the first chapter. Most adolescents want their parents to accept them for who they are and celebrate their increasing independence; I call this the supportive parent.

This is a framework for thinking about how parents approach a particular situation, rather than a set of labels meant to describe anything that is permanent or unchangeable. Parents may migrate between quadrants depending on the issue at hand. I'm not arguing that a certain type of parenting yields kids who are damaged versus successful. To be sure, parents often become overinvolved as a response to their kids' challenges, not the other way around. And if you place yourself in any of the quadrants and are generally happy with your relationship with your adolescent, more power to you.

But my impression is that parents who strive to be supportive have positive relationships with their adolescents; they can approach issues without a control agenda and model an expectation of mutual respect. Paradoxically, adolescents are often more willing to follow the advice and direction of supportive parents than those who demand control or obedience. Thus I advise parents who want to be involved in their adolescents' lives to express affection and acceptance while also gently pushing kids to figure out and implement their own ideas and solutions. None of this, in my experience, diminishes a parent's authority.

Motivational Interviewing for Loved Ones

The strategies in this book are adapted from a therapeutic practice called motivational interviewing (MI). Psychologists William Miller and Stephen Rollnick created motivational interviewing in the 1980s, and since then there have been hundreds of studies evaluating its effects. Overall the research shows that when therapists use MI, patients are more likely to make healthy changes in their lives such as reducing drug and alcohol use, quitting smoking, or adhering to prescribed medications. Although most of this research has involved MI delivered by psychologists, nurses, physicians, or other professionals, you don't need clinical expertise to understand the philosophy or technique.

MI emerged from a tradition of what psychologist Carl Rogers defined as person-centered psychotherapy. The Rogerian model of psychotherapy posits that people have an innate desire to discover and fulfill their own potential. Rogerian therapy strives to create a warm and nonjudgmental relationship through which patients gradually uncover and pursue their own goals. The therapist doesn't tell the patient what to do; rather, she communicates unconditional admiration and acceptance, which in turns allows the patient to shed ambivalence and neurosis in favor of self-improvement and lovingkindness. Describing his model, Rogers wrote, "the curious paradox is that when I accept myself just as I am, then I change." In other words, it is only through a nondirective and nonjudgmental relationship (either with oneself or a therapist) that change becomes possible.

This stands in contrast to cognitive behavioral therapy or CBT, in which the therapist takes a more active, expert role in helping the patient to identify and catalog her thoughts, feelings, and behaviors and understand how these influence one another. Cognitive behavioral therapists do not assume a nondirective stance: they communicate expectations, assign homework, and make recommendations about how patients should challenge thoughts, manage emotions, and tweak behaviors. These recommendations are based in research: for example, since studies have found that people who go to bed at the same time each night are less likely to suffer from insomnia, a CBT therapist will strongly advise patients suffering from insomnia to adopt this behavior.

Motivational interviewing sits in between the person-centered and cognitive-behavioral traditions. It was created by psychologists who felt that a nonjudgmental approach that was nonetheless intently focused on the possibility of changing present-day behaviors would be most effective for helping patients struggling with addiction and other difficulties. Like Rogerian therapists, MI practitioners mostly withhold their own opinion and instead center the conversation on their patients' ambivalence and desires. Similar to Rogerian psychotherapy, the goal of motivational interviewing is to positively influence another person's behavior through partnership rather than authoritarian coercion or behavioral manipulations. But like cognitive behavioral therapy, MI mostly focuses on specific, present-day behaviors. MI therapists listen intently for signals that their patients might be ready to make a change—to drink less, wake up earlier, look for a job, or get to the gym. Once an MI therapist is confident that a patient is interested in change, she will strongly encourage her patient to go for it and will help to problem-solve any potential barriers that might arise.

I call my approach motivational interviewing for loved ones. I don't want parents to be their kids' therapists, to analyze them, or to create treatment plans. I know that parents, unlike MI therapists, cannot withhold judgment and opinions all the time; we love our kids too much, and have too much invested in the outcomes of their choices, to sit on the sidelines. So I've taken the most important concepts from motivational interviewing, simplified the core skills so that anyone can understand and implement them, and adapted each strategy so that it fits into typical family conversations and dynamics. Parents of adolescents can use these skills to convey the spirit of motivational interviewing, which is essentially this: *Tell me more. I believe in you. We can figure this out together.*

Who Controls Your Child's Behavior?

Here's a simple fact. As your children get older, you will have less and less control over all aspects of their lives and behavior. By age ten, kids choose their friends. By fifteen, they probably have romantic interests you know nothing about. At seventeen, they are certain to have friends who are struggling with substance abuse—as well as opportunities to partake themselves. By the time your children are twenty-one, there is little you can do to stop them from visiting a casino, getting a new credit card, marrying someone you don't like, converting to a new religion, or voting for a political candidate you despise. Like it or not, your child's independence is preordained.

What you are left with, mom/dad/grandma/stepmom/uncle, are opinions. Feelings. It's humiliating, I know. Take a moment to scream into your pillow at the absurdity of the situation. Your lovely child, who may be totally financially dependent on you, and who just yesterday came to you upset because they accidentally bought $200 concert tickets from a scam website, is smart enough to blow past any constraints you attempt to install on their electronic devices, determined enough to sink the mood of any family gathering if they are upset, and impulsive enough to "forget" to reply to your *Where are you?* text until three a.m.

But these scenarios are merely possible, not inevitable. You can't control your adolescent's behavior, but you do have considerable power. If you lay the groundwork for a relationship of mutual respect, clear communication, and reasonable expectations, you can increase your influence and avoid most power struggles.

Political scientists describe power as hard or soft. Hard power is getting others to do what you want them to through coercion (threats of punishment) or inducements (money or other rewards). Soft power is getting other people to want what you want. In international politics, soft power accrues when we host the Olympics, invite foreign students to learn at local universities, and export our movies, pop music, and favorite foods.

Which type of power do you have? Which type do you use? Parents sometimes worry that they have little leverage, implicitly identifying coercive control as the only type of influence that is likely to be successful. Most parents do flex hard power from time to time, in the form of rewards and punishments, with varying degrees of success. Young children are usually responsive to the opportunity to earn a sticker or gummy bear by sharing a toy or peeing in the toilet, and they are more likely to refrain from hitting friends because they know they will get a time-out rather than because they comprehend the abstract morality behind the rule. However, our ability to influence behavior through rewards and punishments (what psychologists call contingencies) typically weakens as children grow into teens and young adults. Maybe taking away Ava's phone for a week will show her that you're serious about talking back. Maybe you can get Michael to attend class by threatening to withhold next semester's tuition unless he maintains a B average. These types of contingencies make sense in the abstract but can backfire with older kids by escalating conflict and inhibiting communication. Ever since you took the phone, Ava won't look you in the eye, and Michael's gone monosyllabic since you made the tuition threat. Now you have no idea what's going on with either of them.

Most parents would rather not use inducements (paying money for passing exams) or coercion (no Wi-Fi until the laundry is put away) forever; life is so much easier when multiple generations can agree that good grades and a clean house are goals worth pursuing. It would be even better if your adolescent somehow found you to be a credible source of expert guidance, but most parents who come to my clinic tell me that their kids shrug off well-intentioned advice. Though we love the idea of dispensing wisdom to the youth in their lives, adolescents usually are not interested.

So what are parents to do? Throw up their hands and allow adolescents to make their own decisions (and mistakes)? Not entirely. Rather than coercion or advice, I recommend partnership as the model for parents hoping to influence adolescents' thinking and behavior. In a partnership, your influence comes from the strength of your relationship and your child's willingness to talk to you and accept your input. Partnership may involve asking questions, brainstorming solutions, or just listening attentively as adolescents think through their dilemmas. The following case examples illustrate the difference between power struggle, passivity, and partnership.

Stephen and Ryan

Stephen is a single dad to Ryan, who is a junior in high school. It's a real source of shame and disbelief for Stephen that Ryan has developed a problem with marijuana. Ryan's grades are terrible, and he got kicked off the football team for coming to practice high. Stephen doesn't want to mess around: he's let Ryan know that he'll be administering urine tests at home every Friday and that Ryan will not see the keys to the family's truck again until he can pass a drug test. So every Friday for the past three months, they've performed the same grim ritual. Ryan wordlessly hands the cup of pee to his father, the test is always positive for recent marijuana use, and the truck remains parked in the driveway. Ryan and Stephen are both demoralized by this situation and avoiding each other most of the time. What happened to the cheerful kid who used to draw out football plays for his father at the kitchen table after dinner?

Jasmine and Khalil

Jasmine is the mother of nineteen-year-old Khalil. She's raised her son in a densely populated suburb, quite a different upbringing than her own in a small Caribbean town where everyone knew their neighbors and (mostly) followed the edicts of their elders. Khalil has struggled with depression and loneliness, and Jasmine worries about him every day. She wants nothing more than for him to be happy, loved, and outgoing. But she notices that his loneliness leads to questionable judgment. Today he announced that he's arranged to hang out with friends he's interacted with only through social media. The supposed meetup is an hour away. These people could be literally anyone. Drug dealers, scammers: Jasmine's imagination conjures horrific scenarios. On top of that, Khalil will be in an unfamiliar town, full of unfamiliar people. Who knows how they will perceive her son, a tall, dark-skinned kid with braids and stud earrings? How will he deal with the social or romantic rejection that likely awaits?

Filled with dread, Jasmine considers her options: Forbid Khalil from leaving the house? She's done that before and knows it's a road to nowhere. They'll argue, he'll withdraw in anger—and next time he won't tell her about his plans before he's out the door. She plans instead to stay out of his way and manage her worry with a crossword puzzle, a glass of wine, and a prayer to keep him safe.

Carolina, Antonio, and Anna

Carolina and Antonio are mom and stepdad to Anna, fifteen. Anna is academically gifted and takes advanced classes with older students. Two senior girls invited Anna to attend a weekend ski trip with them. Between the cost of the trip and the lack of supervision, Carolina and Antonio feel strongly that this is a bad idea. But rather than leading with *no*, they encourage Anna to share more details about the trip, her new friends, and her own feelings about the invitation. By listening carefully, they learn that she doesn't care much about the skiing and feels a bit anxious about the cost, but she really likes these girls and is flattered to be included. Carolina listens carefully before speaking. "It sounds like these girls are worth getting to know," she tells Anna, "but the ski trip is not a good fit right now. How else could you spend time with them?" Anna proposes inviting her classmates for an afternoon hike in a wooded park near their town on a different weekend.

Antonio volunteers to chauffer and host the friends for dinner after the hike. Anna is satisfied with this resolution and relieved by her parents' nonjudgmental reaction to her request.

The Fundamentals of Effectiveness Partnership

In the first example, Stephen and Ryan were locked in a power struggle that they both felt they were losing. Jasmine decided on a passive approach because she didn't see a way to talk to Khalil about her concerns without setting off a power struggle. Carolina and Antonio exemplified partnership by soliciting their daughter's opinions, honoring her desire to pursue friendships, and helping Anna find a way forward.

Adolescents—and the rest of us, frankly—trust people who help them feel understood, confident, and in control. Imagine partnership as a table that rests on these three legs. If any of the legs is short or broken, the table collapses. Attend to each leg, and partnership abides.

The *understood* leg falls apart when judgments or assumptions are made—when kids don't have the chance to explain their feelings and dilemmas. Even if you think you already know what your child is going through, if he doesn't have the chance to express himself, he will likely feel misunderstood. You can strengthen this leg by withholding judgment, asking questions, and repeating back what you heard to make sure you got it right. Anna's parents helped her feel understood by asking questions and reflecting her enthusiasm for her new friends.

The *confident* leg wobbles when you ask someone to do something that feels too hard. I might have a sincere wish to exercise more often, but if you invite me to run a marathon with you, the answer will be no: I'm certainly not ready for *that*. Ryan, the high school junior with the marijuana habit, may lack the confidence to quit cold turkey, but he might not be able to admit that to his dad or even himself. You can also inadvertently undermine confidence by jumping in too soon to solve the problem, giving unsolicited advice, or worrying and catastrophizing about worst-case scenarios. When we over-worry or jump in to fix a problem without being asked, we imply that we don't think our kids can figure out the solutions on their own. In contrast, by asking Anna how she could pursue friendships with her classmates without going on the ski trip, Carolina and Antonio showed confidence in her judgment and problem-solving abilities.

Finally, the *in control* leg is critical for the partnership table's stability. People will make truly terrible decisions just to prove that they are in control. Remember the movie *Finding Nemo*? It's Nemo's first day of school, and his nervous dad, Marlin, hovers just out of sight as the kids dare each other to swim past the safety of the coral reef and into open water. Marlin suddenly jumps into the scene to tell Nemo, in front of his friends, that he better not even *think* about it.

Nemo doesn't seem like the daring type, but he is so humiliated by his dad's outburst that he swims out to the forbidden ocean *just to show he can.* And then Nemo gets scooped up by nosy human divers because (of course) his dad was right. Moral of the story? Don't be Marlin! You want your child to accept your advice, not try to prove you wrong.

The aim of many disciplinary strategies is to prove that the parent, not the adolescent, is in control. The method typically involves taking away a coveted item or restricting teenagers' privacy. Physical punishments— hitting kids or making them do physically demanding or painful tasks—also follow this philosophy, only more aggressively. These strategies certainly prove that the adult is stronger and more powerful. But by design, they make kids feel small and out of control, which degrades the potential for mature partnership. This seems completely backward to me. In my experience adolescents may seem regretful and submissive in the moment when these punishments are handed down, but they are usually most upset about getting caught. The aim of discipline should be to ensure that kids use better judgment next time, not that they take more care to cover their tracks and avoid their parents' oversight.

There is a lot we can do to help kids feel in control, starting with listening, taking them seriously, asking for their ideas, and knowing when it's time to back off from a given topic. You can also label your advice *as advice,* as in *Can I offer you some advice?* These are all strategies to try in everyday situations, not just when kids are in trouble.

If that all makes sense but you're not sure how to implement these principles, keep reading. By using reflections, asking great questions, and encouraging your adolescent to find and implement their own solutions, you can avoid power struggles and establish a more respectful relationship. But first it helps to appreciate why this is so hard to do.

Hard Talk Highlights

- Parents can be both understanding and authoritative.

- Supportive parents express affection and acceptance while also gently pushing kids to figure out and implement their own ideas and solutions.

- Adolescents trust people who help them feel understood, confident, and in control.

- The aim of discipline should be to ensure that kids use better judgment next time, not that they take more care to cover their tracks and avoid their parents' oversight.

- Parents aren't therapists, but they can use the skills and philosophy of motivational interviewing to build partnership with adolescents.

CHAPTER 3
THE RIGHTING REFLEX

The righting reflex is a concept from motivational interviewing. It's a name for the near-universal impulse to help people who are in distress by trying to fix their problems, giving them advice, or minimizing their concerns. We do these things for a simple reason: we hate to see people get stuck, feel upset, or do dumb things. It's like a reflex because it's an automatic response to other people's suffering. The righting reflex is not a character flaw or a personality disorder. If you care about people, you probably have a righting reflex.

Although well-intentioned, the righting reflex can get in the way of partnership and healthy change. It weakens all three of your table legs. Think of the righting reflex as an inept carpenter. He reaches for one tool, then another, then another—but his tools don't work at all. After an hour of watching him tinker, the legs are weaker and wobblier, and you feel more helpless than ever. His useless tools are *trying to fix it*, *giving advice*, and *minimizing the issue*.

I always ask parents to think of a time when someone gave them advice or tried to fix their problem in an unhelpful way. They regale me with stories of meddling in-laws, micromanaging bosses, and simpletons who impatiently point out obvious solutions to complicated interpersonal dramas. *So you know what I'm talking about,* I say. *You've been the object of someone's righting reflex. Is it possible that your child sometimes perceives you in a similar way?*

Most parents feel that my characterization is not quite fair. After all, wouldn't it be cruel to withhold helpful information from floundering teens? Is life experience worth nothing? Others claim to be self-effacing, ego-free parents who never give unsolicited advice, since they already know that their kids find them annoying. But I usually find that upon further exploration of the issue, most parents do eventually identify how the righting reflex manifests and creates problems in their family. Consider how this plays out in the following case examples.

Roopa, Priya, Aarav, and Grandma

Roopa, a ninth grader, has been the target of cyberbullies for several weeks. Every time she posts on social media, a horde of anonymous commenters appears and writes that she is ugly, uncool, hopeless, horrible. She fears that these commenters may be classmates but she has no real idea. She has not talked to her parents, Priya and Aarav, or her grandmother about her problem because even though she knows they love her and want to be involved, she suspects they will not be helpful. Yesterday the comments escalated from general insults to specific threats sent to her privately, such as *You better not get caught alone* and *We're always watching you.* She is unsettled and wants to talk to an adult.

ROOPA: I'm so stressed!
PRIYA: Oh, sweetie. Don't stress. I'll make you a snack. You can watch TV.
ROOPA: Uh, never mind. I'm not hungry.

ROOPA: Every time I go on Instagram I feel horrible.
AARAV: I told you that stuff is all trash. You should delete your account. You spend too much time on there anyway.
ROOPA: You're so judgmental!

ROOPA: Nani, people are saying mean things about me.
GRANDMA: Don't worry about what other people think. You are special.
ROOPA: Okay, thanks . . .

The adults who care about Roopa let their righting reflex get in the way of hearing her. Roopa tried to confide in them, but when she looked for signals that the adults in her house were receptive, all she found was noise. Mom tried to fix the problem by offering snacks and TV. Dad gave unsolicited advice that is probably the exact opposite of what Roopa really ought to do: by deleting her account, she'd likely lose any chance of figuring out who is behind the threats.

Grandma minimized the issue, telling Roopa not to worry so much. None of them got far enough into a real conversation to understand the nature of Roopa's problem. None of them gave her any confidence that she could find her way through it or helped her to feel in control of the solution.

Now, imagine that these three adults were able to support Roopa without letting the righting reflex get in the way. The conversation might have gone something like this.

ROOPA: Mom, I'm so stressed!

PRIYA: ~~Let me fix you a snack.~~ Why?

ROOPA: Everyone hates me.

PRIYA: ~~I'm sure that's not true.~~ What makes you say that?

ROOPA: Look at these messages I'm getting. They're really messed up.

PRIYA: ~~Give me your phone, I'm showing this to your teacher.~~ Oh, wow. I'm glad you showed this to me. Aarav, come here.

AARAV: What?

PRIYA: Look at these horrible messages someone sent to Roopa.

AARAV: ~~See? I knew she was too young for a phone. This is unacceptable.~~ What on earth? When did this start?

ROOPA: Well, a few weeks ago I posted a selfie. Then someone whose username I didn't recognize posted "ugly bitch." See, I'll show you. Okay, so then a bunch of random people requested to follow me. And then it just piled on. See? And then yesterday, they started DM'ing me.

AARAV: ~~I warned you about posting selfies. And why would you let strangers see your posts? It's like you're not thinking.~~ Whoa, we had no idea you were dealing with this. Pretty scary.

ROOPA: I didn't want to worry you.

PRIYA: ~~Promise you'll come to me sooner next time!~~ It's okay, we can help you figure this out. I'd like to talk to the principal of your school. And we should probably make some rules about what you post and who you allow to see your posts. What do you think of that?

ROOPA: Yeah, I guess that makes sense. I just— *(she starts to cry and trails off)*

GRANDMA: Roopa, ~~don't cry!~~ what's wrong?

ROOPA: Um, I don't know, people are just being so mean!

GRANDMA: ~~I'm sure they are nice once you get to know them.~~ Kids can be terrible. Tell me everything.

See the difference? In this version, Roopa's family was not indifferent or distant. But they also hung back for just a beat to learn more about her problem before trying to fix it, giving advice, or waving her away. They didn't criticize her for not coming to them sooner or for using poor judgment on social media. They helped her feel understood (by asking questions and looking at the posts and messages), confident (by affirming that she's done the right thing in coming to them), and in control (by believing her and asking what she thinks about their suggestions). The sense of partnership is strong.

It's easy to feel sorry for Roopa, who is clearly a victim and needs some adult guidance. It can be harder to apply these concepts when kids are being defiant and disrespectful. But even though they are more challenging to connect with, defiant and aloof kids need partnership too.

Mark and David

Mark graduated from college a few months ago. He's having trouble finding a job in his field, for reasons that are fairly obvious to his parents. He has let his hair and beard grow shaggy, seems contemptuous of the job leads his parents suggest, and in general is acting like a bit of a jerk these days. He comes into the kitchen in his pajamas one morning at ten o'clock, clearly in a bad mood, and encounters his father, David.

DAVID: Good morning, Mark.

MARK: Oh, hey.

DAVID: What are your plans today?

MARK: I don't know. Nothing. I didn't get that job I interviewed for last week.

DAVID: You just need to keep applying for things. Focus on volume—at least one application every day. And let me take you shopping. You can't wear those old sneakers to interviews. I warned you those would make a bad impression. A haircut would go a long way too. Chin up, son.

MARK: You're such an asshole! You don't know anything about programming jobs.

DAVID: You know what, I'm sick of your attitude! Your mother and I have done nothing but support you.

Poor David. All he offered was sound advice, new clothes, and a rent-free place to stay. Unfortunately, Mark is in a vulnerable spot, psychologically speaking. His confidence has taken a hit. He hears his dad's advice as criticism about a sensitive topic, salt in the wound of fresh rejection. Imagine if David had tamped down his righting reflex and tried a different approach.

DAVID: What are your plans today, Mark?

MARK: I don't know. Nothing. I didn't get that job I interviewed for last week.

DAVID: Oh, bummer. I know you were excited about that one.

MARK: It's so hard to keep going sometimes, you know? I feel like I worked so hard for my degree, but it's not worth anything in the real world.

DAVID: Yeah, I've felt that way.

MARK: I don't know, maybe I'm applying to the wrong positions.

DAVID: Can I give you some advice?

MARK: I guess so.

DAVID: I know I'm old-fashioned, but I think a new interview suit and a haircut could go a long way. At least you might feel more confident.

MARK: I don't know, the culture of programmers is super casual. I don't think they care that much whether you wear a suit. But I guess a haircut couldn't hurt. My beard is kind of nasty, isn't it?

DAVID: Well, I've definitely seen it looking better!

Reining in the righting reflex made a big difference here. By showing sympathy and understanding *before* making suggestions, and by asking permission before sharing his ideas about how to fix the problem, David was able to give advice successfully. The conversation stayed positive; Mark and his father are on the same team.

One of the most interesting things about the righting reflex is how it often has the opposite impact from what the "helper" intended. David's initial advice—chin up, act on the things you can control, keep going—sounded positive, but the impact was souring. Mark felt criticized and defensive, and thus disregarded the advice completely. On the other hand, words that sound negative—bummer, I've been there—somehow elicited the opposite reaction. Mark was open to his father's suggestions because he felt understood. He didn't need to defend his approach or his character.

Sophie, Tara, and Kate

Some parents tell me about adolescents who lean excessively on their involvement and advice rather than rejecting their input. This is often a longstanding pattern that is difficult to disrupt. On the one hand, parents enjoy their kids' affection and respect. On the other, they are frustrated by their kids' lack of drive and self-sufficiency. These parents aren't so much inserting their unsolicited opinions as responding to their kids' explicit requests for assistance. Even so, the righting reflex exists, in that parents feel awful withholding reassurance and help to kids who have come to rely on it. At the same time older adolescents may feel stuck and embarrassed or resentful about how dependent they are on their parents.

For example, Sophie is a first-semester college student who has always been close to her mothers. She calls Tara and Kate throughout the day, often just to chat, but sometimes for input on decisions large and small. Tara usually likes it when Sophie calls to check in, but sometimes she works an overnight nursing shift and silences her phone when she gets home in the morning so that she can get some uninterrupted sleep. Here is what the righting reflex sounds like in this family.

TARA: Hey, Sophie, what's up? Why did you call three times?

SOPHIE: Why didn't you pick up?

TARA: I've told you that I can't always talk on the phone in the mornings. What's going on?

SOPHIE: Okay, okay, I'll be quick. I need to talk to you because today is the last day to drop classes without penalty, and I can't decide whether to drop my painting elective. It's super fun but it's at eight thirty in the morning and I've been staying up late to get all the writing done for freshman comp and then having to be in class at eight thirty just, like, sucks.

TARA: Drop it then—you certainly don't need it for premed and it sounds like it's stressing you out.

SOPHIE: But Mom! I think I should stay with it because it's just so cool to take a painting class and also one of the painting majors invited me to this gallery opening and party.

TARA: Well, you asked me what I think, and I told you.

SOPHIE: Oh my god! I'm just trying to talk to you.

TARA: Listen, if you wake me up to ask for my advice, you can't get upset with me for giving it. It's not a big deal whether you drop your class or not. Stop worrying so much about it.

Tara was understandably frustrated by this conversation because Sophie woke her up, demanded advice, and then got upset about Tara's opinion. Only after she heard Tara's reaction did Sophie realize that she wasn't quite ready to make a decision. Tara's righting reflex came in the form of acquiescing to Sophie's request for advice, and then telling her not to worry so much. Neither of them was happy about how this conversation went. Let's remove the righting reflex and give Tara another chance.

TARA: Hey, Sophie, what's up? Why did you call three times?

SOPHIE: Why didn't you pick up?

TARA: I've told you that I can't always talk on the phone in the mornings. What's going on?

SOPHIE: I need to talk to you because today is the last day to drop classes without penalty and I can't decide whether to drop my painting elective. It's super fun but it's at eight thirty in the morning and I've been staying up late to get all the writing done for freshman comp and then having to be in class at eight thirty just, like, sucks.

TARA: Tough decision.

SOPHIE: Yeah, I hate getting up early, but I feel like if I were more organized, then I wouldn't be staying up so late and it would all be more manageable. Plus, I really am getting a lot out of the class. The professor is amazing and one of the painting majors invited me to this gallery opening and party.

TARA: So on the one hand it would be a relief not to have to get up early, but on the other hand you love the class and would be sad to drop it.

SOPHIE: Exactly.

TARA: When do you need to decide?

SOPHIE: By noon. Which is . . . oh, jeez . . . in fifteen minutes.

TARA: That's not much time! What would you have to do if you decided to drop the class?

SOPHIE: It's easy, you just log into the system and unenroll. But you know what? I think I haven't dropped it yet because deep down I want to make it work.

TARA: You do sound excited about it.

SOPHIE: I just have to be better about getting right to work after dinner to do my writing assignments. Thanks, Mom. Sorry for waking you up. I'll let you go back to sleep.

TARA: I'll try my best. Bye, hon.

In this conversation, Tara admirably overpowered any righting reflex. She avoided offering advice and instead helped Sophie think about her own priorities. She didn't tell her daughter not to worry; instead, she validated that Sophie was facing a difficult decision. Rather than giving into her righting reflex, Tara used simple tools called reflections and open-ended questions to help Sophie arrive at a decision. I'll teach you how to use these in Chapters 4 and 5.

Resisting Righting

Even once you understand the concept of the righting reflex and how it gets in the way of partnership, learning to recognize and control this impulse in real time is exceedingly difficult. We all have themes that trigger our righting reflex; for some it's money, or weight loss, or mental health, or academics. Everyone has that topic that they just can't resist giving advice about, often because it's something that you have struggled with personally and you want to share your hard-won wisdom. And if you are a teacher or a hairdresser or a nurse or a lawyer or a salesperson, then your job involves giving advice, and it can be hard to fathom why your own kids are so reluctant to listen to the advice that total strangers pay good money to hear.

Alongside that benevolent desire to share your wisdom, though, lives the universal anxiety about the fact that you can't control anyone's behavior but your own. The righting reflex is a function of both altruism and anxiety. Mastering your righting reflex requires you to accept the reality that your ability to command other people is limited. This is a hard pill to swallow—and it's one that parents must ingest over and over again. The popularity of the line by Elizabeth Stone that to become a parent is "forever to have your heart go walking around outside your body" illustrates the difficulty. Simply put, it is painful and scary to cede control over your child's well-being, which is sometimes impossible to distinguish from your own beating heart.

Recognizing and managing one's own anxiety as it flares is the kind of herculean accomplishment a person can spend years in therapy pursuing. I was probably halfway through graduate school and twenty-seven years old before I began to recognize my own emotions. Most of us can remember a past situation in which we felt sad, happy, worried, angry, or otherwise emotional, but recognizing feelings as they emerge is surprisingly hard to do. Think about all the times when someone asked you if anything was wrong and you gritted your teeth and said "no," "nothing," or "mind your own business." You might have been intentionally stonewalling, but more likely you had no idea how to interpret or articulate the static in your head.

Let me say this plainly: when something important is out of our control, it is normal and healthy to feel nervous, overwhelmed, angry, or upset. This experience can be summarized under the umbrella of "anxiety," but there are many gradations. It's a feeling you might experience when your flight gets canceled, your roof leaks, your blood work comes back with abnormalities, you get an email from your boss with the subject line "we need to meet," or your child's school calls. It feels like the lurch of a roller coaster, blood pressure rising, sweat breaking out, or tension in your forehead. Your response might be to criticize others, defend yourself, cry, run away, or flush with embarrassment.

Anxiety is hard to describe in universal terms because everyone experiences it a bit differently. Try to remember what you felt like and how you reacted the last time you were hit by something unexpected and overwhelming. Notice what happens to your body and mood the next time a situation like that arises. You can only manage your anxiety if you have the self-awareness to know that it's happening.

It surprises people to learn that anxiety and rage are first cousins, but if you work backward from rage, you can often find fear as the underlying experience that triggers the emotional cascade toward anger. That man yelling at the nurse in the hospital hallway is scared that his mother is going to die. The woman demanding to speak with a manager is afraid that the home repair she needs is going to bankrupt her family. And the parents scolding their teenager, yelling and pointing and threatening to withhold phones and money and transportation and internet, are terrified that they can't protect her.

Learning to recognize your anxiety response is a liberating experience. You can feel your anxiety and instead of thinking *this is an emergency!* you will instead think *ah yes, this is what it feels like to be alive in an uncontrollable world.* You will still experience the horrible urgency of your worries, wants, and longing for control, but you will have more freedom to choose how you want to respond to those feelings. You can take a few minutes to center yourself before reacting to whatever has triggered your anxiety. This is sometimes called mindfulness. In practice, responding mindfully might mean taking a slow, deep breath, going for a walk around the block, or texting a friend to say "I'm so overwhelmed."

When your child has triggered an anxiety response, it's difficult to remember the concept of the righting reflex, your intention to control it, or how you might do that. However, if you can learn to recognize and manage that anxiety, you will have your whole brain at your disposal. You will remember that you read this book and that you resolved to try something new. If you can't manage your anxiety, you probably won't remember any of the strategies laid out in the next few chapters until the moment to use them has passed.

So next time you find your righting reflex activated by your child's dilemma or behavior, or you feel upset or enraged by something he's said or done, try to recognize that emotion. Acknowledge it and cope with it. Notice your instinct to fix the problem, give advice, or minimize the issue, and put it gently aside. Instead, try responding with a *hmm, what's going on,* or *tell me more.* If you absolutely cannot resist giving feedback or advice, try asking if your teen wants to hear it before you share. You can say, *Are you looking for advice?, Can I share some ideas?,* or *I've been through something similar. Can I tell you about what I learned?* If he turns down your advice, then you know that he isn't in a good place to hear or follow it, so it's truly better if you save that wisdom for another time. And once you've read the next chapters, you will be equipped with more great alternatives to the righting reflex.

Hard Talk Highlights

- The righting reflex is the near-universal impulse to help people who are in distress by trying to fix their problems, giving them advice, or minimizing their concerns.

- Although well-intentioned, the righting reflex can get in the way of partnership and healthy change.

- Everyone has topics that they just can't resist giving advice about, often because it's something they have struggled with personally, so they want to share their hard-won wisdom.

- Notice your instinct to fix the problem, give advice, or minimize the issue, and put it gently aside. Instead, try responding with a *hmm, what's going on,* or *tell me more.*

CHAPTER 4
REFLECTIONS

Once you become aware of your righting reflex, you may find yourself at a loss for words. If you want to avoid giving advice or offering reassurance, what can you say? In the next two chapters I'll describe the two fundamental tools of motivational interviewing: reflections and open-ended questions. These are the basics that you'll need in order to move away from a righting response toward a more empowering and productive conversation.

Reflections are the first building block. Reflections slow down a conversation and help you focus on listening. A good reflection holds up a mirror so that your adolescent knows you can hear and see him, feels important and respected, and has the chance to think more deeply about what he said. When you are on the receiving end of a thoughtful reflection, you usually keep talking, because it feels so good to have an attentive audience.

So how do you do a reflection? First, relax your voice into a tone that is nonjudgmental and accepting. A reflection is a statement, not a question, so the pitch of your voice must gently drop at the end of the sentence. And here's what you say: you repeat back what your child just said (simple reflection), summarize or guess at what your child meant (complex reflection), or name the underlying emotion that your child is expressing (feelings reflection).

To be effective, reflections must be free of judgment. When you do a reflection, you don't show whether you agree or disagree; you don't evaluate what your child is saying as good or bad at all. In this way, reflections are different from praise, because praise is inherently evaluative (a positive judgment). Praise says, *Good job! I approve.* A reflection says, *I hear you. I understand.*

That is all a bit abstract, so let's go back to Roopa from Chapter 3, who is dealing with cyberbullies, and her mom, Priya. Priya's response was steered by her righting reflex. But rather than trying to fix Roopa's problem, Priya will practice using three types of reflections.

ROOPA: I think half the kids in my grade must have made fake accounts just to call me ugly.
PRIYA: Half your grade is calling you names. *(simple reflection)*

OR:

PRIYA: It seems like so many kids are involved. *(complex reflection)*

OR:

PRIYA: That sounds very hurtful. *(feelings reflection)*

Notice that Priya does not point out that the comments might be made by one individual with many fake profiles, nor does she provide any reassurance, advice, or solutions. Instead, in all three examples, she reflects Roopa's statement briefly and then stops talking. This keeps Roopa and her problem in the spotlight so that she can continue to think and talk about the situation. None of the reflection types (simple, complex, or feelings) is necessarily the correct approach; all three work well to communicate understanding and encourage Roopa to continue to confide in Priya.

Priya's reflections are also effective because they are brief. Many parents I work with struggle with this aspect of the skill. They offer a reflection, but then they want to continue talking. They pad their reflection with a lot of other speech. If you are new to the skill, it can feel unnatural or insufficient to let a reflection sit and take up space in a conversation. And if your child takes a moment to think before replying, anxiety creeps in. Silence, even for a moment, can be awkward. When you are nervous about what your child might say next, five seconds feels like an hour. But it is important to pause for a moment after a reflection, if only to see whether your child wants to correct or add anything to your understanding of their dilemma.

The other difficult part of doing good reflections is that you must temporarily put aside any agenda. The goal is simply to show understanding and attention. Even if your child expresses an opinion that you disagree with or makes a statement that is not accurate, a reflection does not debate the accuracy or merit of the statement. If you want to, you can return to the point later to share your own alternative perspective. To do a reflection, you have to slow down, listen to your child's side of the story, and delay for a moment your own goal of sharing information or giving advice. Parents whose kids barely talk to them often feel an urgent need to spit out advice before they lose their adolescents' attention: this book is about moving past this dynamic completely.

Here is an example. Recall Mark (the recent college graduate) and his father, David, from Chapter 3. Mark is slogging through job applications, and he complains to his dad about the process. David is eager to see Mark succeed in his job search and privately thinks that Mark could be working harder toward this goal. He checks in with Mark about his progress.

DAVID: How is the job search going?

MARK: Cover letters are so dumb. Can't someone just look at my resume and decide whether I'm qualified for a job? Why do I have to write a whole essay about how some entry-level position is my dream job?

DAVID: Cover letters are important—it's how you show a potential employer that you understand the nature of the job and you have the background to do it.

MARK: I know, I know. This whole process is exhausting.

DAVID: Once you have a job, you'll be working eight-hour days. In the meantime, a lot of people treat searching for a job like that's their full-time job.

Mark rolls his eyes and walks away.

Cover letters are important. David meant well, but this was not a reflection. In fact, it refuted what Mark just said. Mark likely felt patronized by his father's attempt to teach him something when he was seeking a sympathetic ear. David came off as pedantic and awkward, which isn't what he intended. A parent once told me that she was always looking for teachable moments, but as we worked together, she realized she could help her son more by finding listenable moments instead. Let's have David treat this conversation as a listenable moment by using reflections.

MARK: Cover letters are so dumb. Can't someone just look at my resume and decide whether I'm qualified? Why do I have to write a whole essay about how some entry-level position is my dream job?

DAVID: You feel like cover letters are dumb. *(simple reflection)*

MARK: I mean, I guess the employer wants to know, like, whether you actually read the job description and can put a few sentences together coherently.

DAVID: It's a bit of a test, I suppose. *(complex reflection)*

MARK: Yeah, and I'm so sick of writing them.

DAVID: Sounds exhausting. *(feelings reflection)*

MARK: I just need to get through two more today, and then I'm going to take a break and meet up with Sam for a drink.

DAVID: Good luck!

In this example, David used all three types of reflection—simple, complex, and feelings—instead of arguing. With each of the statements, David held up a mirror so that Mark could experience David's uncritical attention and hear how his words sound in the voice of another person. It wasn't exactly flattering to hear his thoughts reflected. Hearing their own words and feelings reflected back to them sometimes helps adolescents and young adults adopt a more mature attitude and make peace with the tasks ahead of them. In this scenario Mark didn't need a lecture from his dad about the importance of cover letters; once he heard his (somewhat obnoxious) view reflected back to him, he corrected himself on the subject. And David got to learn that Mark is indeed working on multiple applications, easing his worries about Mark's productivity.

Some parents worry that using a reflection in this situation implies that they agree with or support their adolescent's ill-informed opinion. When David said *you feel like cover letters are dumb*, he wasn't representing it as his own perspective, but he didn't argue against it either. He simply withheld his own opinion and reflected Mark's. Mark was not confused by this: he was perfectly aware that it wasn't David's opinion, but rather than debating his dad, he reconsidered his own silly statement. David's use of the words *you feel like* helped to put some additional daylight between Mark's statement and David's own worldview.

Skeptical parents, or those whose children have truly terrible judgment, might wonder if it's realistic to expect that a reflection or two can prompt adolescents to talk themselves out of their worst ideas. That skepticism is reasonable. Sometimes a reflection does not get you there. But doing the reflecting is still important, because if your child continues to advocate for bad ideas or unrealistic plans, then you will need to give advice. And if you give advice without first demonstrating that you've tried to understand your adolescent's perspective, your advice will irritate, fall flat, or be dismissed.

Think back to the conversation that David and Mark had about going to see a barber before his next job interview. Mark needed his dad's advice—he wasn't going to arrive at the realization that he should get a haircut on his own. But when David offered the advice too soon, Mark rejected it. When David first tried a feelings reflection and indicated that he understood Mark's dilemma—*bummer, I know you were excited*—Mark was much more receptive.

Back Talk

It may seem logical enough to try to use reflections when your adolescent's frustration is aimed toward an external target—online bullies, or the stultifying composition of cover letters, for example. But for most of the parents I work with, it's a much harder sell when I propose that reflections are just as useful when the target is *them*.

To put it mildly, reactions to back talk are complicated. Your reaction might be informed by your cultural background, your own upbringing, your mood, and who happens to be watching. Imagine this familiar scenario: you tell your adolescent that it's time to stop scrolling and get going (to school, the store, church, whatever). You are ignored. You repeat your request a second time, and then a third time, loudly and sharply: *Put the phone away and get in the car!* Then, you hear these words coming out of your child's mouth: *Aaargh! I heard you. You are so annoying.*

What would your parents have done? Slapped you across the face? Snatched the phone from your hand? Stormed out of the room and given you the silent treatment? Yelled *I don't appreciate your tone, young lady!*? Laughed it off? Ignored your tone completely and repeated the request? How do you typically respond? Most importantly, are you happy with your approach?

I don't claim to have a correct method for addressing back talk, but I do know that sometimes— especially when a topic is sensitive—it can be worthwhile to set aside the understandable impulse to correct an adolescent's tone if you are working on the long-term goals of partnership and substantive conversations. It's helpful to consider the reason for the back talk or attitude. Most of the time, back talk represents nothing more than grumpiness, the same dumb sniping that you might get into with a spouse about who did or didn't misplace the keys when you're rushing out the door. In these cases, back talk certainly isn't appreciated, but it's also not a major signal of disrespect. These meaningless, fleeting moments of minor rudeness can escalate into major power struggles that drag on for hours, days, or weeks. And power struggles do real harm to the partnership goal, all over something so silly. Parents have only a fraction of a second to choose whether and how to focus on the disrespect or just move on. But it can be a consequential choice.

If you would prefer to move on quickly rather than fighting about tone, a gentle correction can communicate that you don't like the disrespect and get the interaction back on track. Let's go back to the moment outlined previously and see how different responses can either escalate or cool the conflict.

AARAV: Hey, I'm tired of repeating myself. Put your phone down and get in the car.
ROOPA: Aaargh! I heard you. You are so annoying.
AARAV: That's it! No phone for the rest of the day.
ROOPA: I hate you!
AARAV: Oh, really? No phone for the rest of the week!

AARAV: Hey, I'm tired of repeating myself. Put your phone down and get in the car.
ROOPA: Aaargh! I heard you. You are so annoying.
AARAV: Hey, come on now. That hurts my feelings.
ROOPA: Okay, okay, I'm coming.

At other times back talk does contain meaning. For instance, back talk may serve as a defense against perceived criticism (not feeling understood) or pushiness (not feeling in control). In these cases reflections can quickly clear the air. By offering a reflection, you show that you hear your child loud and clear, and you also give her an opportunity to express her point without attitude and sarcasm. Here are some examples of parents using complex reflections to respond to back talk.

TARA: Hey Sophie, when I get home from my shift, I don't want to see the house full of dirty dishes. You're on school break; you're not that busy. Find a few minutes to clean up, okay?
SOPHIE: I have literally no idea what you are even talking about. Jeez.
TARA: You're not sure what I meant by that.
SOPHIE: No, it's fine, I understand. I'll do it.
TARA: Thanks.

DAVID: Mark, have you seen my wallet? There's a lot of money in there.
MARK: Wow, you are so quick to think the worst of me. I can't stand it here.
DAVID: You feel like I'm accusing you! No, seriously, I'm just looking for my wallet. I need cash for the pizza guy.
MARK: Oh—sorry—I haven't seen it. Sorry again.

The parents in these examples are working hard to suppress reflexive anger and sarcasm. Their reflections are calm and sincere. This degree of earnestness takes some practice and self-control, and no one manages to execute it perfectly every time. But when you pull it off, you feel great, because you know you have prevented a spiral of escalating irritation and anger.

Reflections Don't Agree

By now you understand that reflections don't debate or disagree. It's just as important to note that reflections also don't agree. It can be so exciting when your adolescent says something rational, or even wise, that you want to cheer them on. Or you may be scraping for a point of agreement in an otherwise tense conversation. I think that it is lovely and kind to praise your adolescents or let them know that you share their perspective. But praise and agreement are fundamentally different from reflections. For example, if your teen says *I think I need to start going to bed earlier,* your instinct might be to say *that's fantastic!* (praise) or *yes, you should* (agreement). Reflection is a different approach, one that emphasizes your adolescent's own views about her behavior rather than your eagerness to see her comply with your wishes. To do a reflection in this situation, you could say *you're ready to make a change* or *you sound pretty motivated.* For adolescents who tend to bristle at adult authority, this can be a more effective approach.

Reflecting Ambivalence

Let's check in with Stephen and Ryan from Chapter 2. When we last heard from them, they were locked in a miserable routine of drug tests that never came out clean, a punishment with no clear impact and no end in sight, and a wall of frustration building between them.

Stephen knows that his approach isn't working, and he wants to talk with Ryan about this extremely sensitive topic. He's got to know: Why on earth does Ryan continue to use marijuana in spite of the consequences? When the latest drug test comes back positive, Stephen knocks on Ryan's bedroom door to have a hard talk. He is determined to use reflections to learn as much as he can about Ryan's perspective on this problem.

STEPHEN: So . . . you're still smoking.

RYAN: Yeah, whatever. No truck. I know.

STEPHEN: I guess me taking away the truck hasn't made you want to stop.

RYAN: Uh . . . I don't know what to say.

STEPHEN: It's hard to talk about.

RYAN: Well, yeah, obviously you're right. I haven't stopped smoking.

STEPHEN: Okay. Um. Help me understand.

RYAN: Dad, what do you want? My life's just like, fucked now. I'm thrown off football, I can't go anywhere, school sucks. Coming home and relaxing in my room is like, all I have.

STEPHEN: So smoking helps you feel relaxed.

RYAN: Yeah. I look forward to it all day.

STEPHEN: You don't have much else you're excited about.

RYAN: It sounds pathetic but it's my one thing I still like.

STEPHEN: But isn't there any part of you that wants to stop? I mean, all these consequences.

RYAN: Of course. I don't want to be a loser who never does anything.

STEPHEN: So . . . on the one hand, smoking has made you feel like a loser because you're not playing football and you're stuck at home. And on the other hand, marijuana is a positive thing for you because it's the only pleasure in your life right now.

RYAN: Yes. Yes, exactly.

STEPHEN: Gosh, kid, you are in a tough spot. How on earth do we fix this?

RYAN: I don't know. But those tests you do on my pee—I feel like I'll never pass. About a month ago, I didn't smoke for three whole weeks. I was so proud of myself. But the test still came back positive. To be honest with you, I thought about killing myself that night. I mean, I would never do it. But I'm just trying to tell you that I was really trying to make a change. And that set me back.

STEPHEN: I had no idea. Three weeks? You were doing great! I wish you had told me.

RYAN: It's nothing to be proud of.

STEPHEN: I didn't realize there was so much going on in your head about this. I thought you just didn't care. Let me think about this. I don't know what to do, but I'll take some time to think. Thanks for talking to me.

RYAN: Sure. I didn't realize you were interested.

In this conversation, Stephen masterfully used reflections to explore Ryan's complicated feelings about drug use. Ryan disclosed that he feels ambivalent—he wants to quit, but he also wants to use. Ambivalence about change is normal. We don't have to fully resolve or repress our ambivalence to successfully commit to a change. Who hasn't felt tugs of fear and sadness when quitting a job or leaving a relationship? Or a twitch of reluctance when forgoing the couch for the gym? Ryan's ambivalence about his drug use may be a healthy sign that he's ready to make a change.

Notice that Stephen didn't judge Ryan's ambivalence or become frustrated by it. He used a two-sided reflection to capture Ryan's complex feelings and motivations. *On the one hand, smoking has made you feel like a loser because you're not playing football and you're stuck at home. And on the other hand, marijuana is a positive thing for you because it's the only pleasure in your life right now.* This is a great technique to highlight ambivalence and talk about it openly.

From this conversation, Stephen learned a lot of important information. He learned that Ryan isn't feeling understood, confident, or in control. He learned that his son's mental health is seriously suffering. He found out that Ryan has a lot of motivation to stop using—he managed to abstain for three weeks. And he learned that, by failing to appreciate Ryan's small but significant steps toward change, the weekly drug tests may be doing more harm than good.

But Stephen didn't *only* use reflections to steer this hard talk into fruitful territory. He also showed interest through a curious prompt (*help me understand*) and an open-ended question (*how do we fix this?*). These are the other building blocks of motivational interviewing that you will need for a successful hard talk.

Hard Talk Highlights

- Reflections slow down a conversation and help you focus on listening.

- To do a reflection, repeat back what your child just said (simple reflection), summarize or guess at what your child meant (complex reflection), or name the underlying emotion that your child is expressing (feelings reflection).

- To be effective, reflections must be free of judgment. They don't agree or disagree.

- Hearing their own words and feelings reflected back to them sometimes helps adolescents and young adults to adopt a more mature attitude and make peace with the tasks ahead of them.

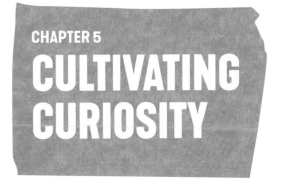

CHAPTER 5

CULTIVATING CURIOSITY

Before our children are born, we have a wondrous sense of the infinite possibilities of their lives. Will they be readers? Musicians? Good cooks? Athletic? Spiritual? Outgoing? Imagining what they might be like is one of the joys of becoming a parent.

As babies become children, our questions inevitably become more prosaic. Is she going to need glasses? Is there anything at this restaurant he might eat? What size shoes do they wear? I don't think this happens because our imaginations are diminished by parenthood. I believe instead, that after the benefit of many hours and years in the presence of our children, we get to know them quite well. We don't need to imagine who they are or could be; we can see them right in front of us, eating a sandwich and bopping around to whatever's playing in their headphones. Rekindling a sense of wonder about teens' inner lives, ambitions, and abilities is an important part of building a partnership as they gain independence.

By the time children become teens, parents' curiosity does not feel so innocent. So much of what preoccupies adolescents makes adults nervous. I'll be explicit: parents desperately want to know if their kids are skipping school, having sex, drinking, or using drugs. Twenty-first-century parents have digital tools like GPS location tracking, cloud-based text and photo backup, surveillance cameras, and debit card transaction records that they can use to satisfy their curiosity and feed their desire for information. Some companies will even alert you in real time if your kid exceeds the speed limit or crosses the town line.

These tools can be useful if your child knows you are using them, and they can be activated as temporary guard rails if your child has demonstrated poor judgment and needs to get back on track. But surreptitious spying on your kids is not compatible with the partnership goal. You will get data, but not context, so there is a high risk that you will not be able to understand or correctly interpret what you are learning. From your adolescent's perspective, being snooped on will not help them to feel understood, confident, or in control. A teen who knows or suspects that they are being surveilled will probably become more secretive and rebellious rather than more open and communicative. Think about your own adolescence: Would you have been better off if your parents had access to constant data about your whereabouts and behavior?

I get it. After enough fruitless efforts at conversation, anyone will eventually give up on the goal of constructive dialogue and seek other ways to deal with adolescents. For many parents, snooping feels safer and easier than conversation. Teens can be real jerks, contemptuous and dismissive of adults' reasonable concerns. They may resent parents' efforts to control and supervise, or they may not think about their parents very much at all. I write from experience; I vividly remember being a teenager myself. I often regarded my own parents as mere furniture, obstacles to be sidestepped on my way out the door.

But alas, awful as your teen may be sometimes, you are the adult, and you have decided to focus on the one thing you can control: your own behavior. Getting your adolescent to talk to you about her behavior and inner life requires you to get curious, set aside your judgment and righting reflex, and manage the anxieties that arise. I'll be blunt: it's not for everyone. Some parents prefer a "don't ask, don't tell" policy when it comes to contentious issues like drug use and sexuality. My advice, as always, is intended only for parents seeking a new approach.

Starting Over

For most parents there is a mournful element to children's increasing independence and growth. We'll never again get to cuddle our chubby-cheeked babies or bounce them until they shriek with glee. Our preschoolers' nonsensical stories and silly dances are all in the past. The tooth fairy has come and gone, as have Santa, Elmo, bedtime stories, and all the other evanescent particulars of the little worlds our children create as they progress through their developmental stages. If all goes well, we wind up with big people instead of little ones, and there is much to celebrate. But the feeling of loss remains. And it can be hard not to resent (just a little) the smug, smelly, sarcastic teenager standing in the spot where an adorable gap-toothed kindergartener once reveled in your attention and companionship.

To have real conversations with your adolescent, you have to be interested in and excited about this new person. Although most parents like the *idea* of getting to know their children, the reality can be a little overwhelming. What if you discover that your children have different political beliefs from you? That they are exploring different religions? That they are having sex? Or that they can't wait to leave their hometown? These realities can be hard to process, and parents often have trouble distinguishing these sincerely held positions from back talk or disrespect. Ironically, parents who insist on a particular worldview or compulsively debate their child's newfound beliefs can inadvertently push their adolescent further into the contrarian stance.

It can also be hard to let go of what you think you know about your child's personality, interests, and talents. The fact is, they are free to change. An outgoing child may become more reserved. A talented athlete might elect to retire from her sport. A one-time Disney princess devotee may announce that they've rejected the gender binary. I'm not saying you must accept these conclusions passively. But rather than assuming that our job is to push our children back to the birthday party or baseball field, we must regard these changes with curiosity and a desire to understand what's behind them.

On a more positive note, the potential fun of getting to know adolescents as individuals cannot be overstated. A few years ago I was at a party hosted by a couple whose children were in high school and college. As the night went on, the kids' friends trickled into the house, and a group of them started playing music—piano, guitar, singing. My own children were young and my interactions with teens typically occur in clinical, inorganic settings, not social events. As the kids sang and danced and joked around, I was enchanted by the talent of the young musicians and the style and energy of their friends. I couldn't believe how old I'd become—old enough to be awed by the dynamism of kids at a house party.

Kids are cool, right? They morph so quickly from awkward and dependent preteens to individuals with a wealth of knowledge and opinions about sports and music and literature and pop culture. They make up slang and experiment with fashion. They are physically adept, in ways that make adults both proud (shooting three-point baskets, landing backflips) and profoundly uncomfortable (scaling fences, skateboarding in questionable settings, having sex). They aren't afraid to throw themselves into new hobbies, romances, and friendships. Their world is so vibrant and unpredictable.

They can stay up all night talking to each other about their ideas.

So why is it so difficult to connect with these people? I think that the challenge for adults is twofold: avoiding assumptions about people you have known intimately for their entire lives, and sustaining nonjudgmental curiosity about their actual behaviors and opinions. This challenge has a deeply spiritual dimension. Zen Buddhism emphasizes the concept of beginner's mind, the effort to sustain openness and avoid preconceptions despite having a great deal of expertise. Although we know our children intimately, practicing beginner's mind helps us to ask good questions and listen earnestly to the answers we hear. Similarly, the Jewish philosopher Rabbi Abraham Joshua Heschel described the concept of radical amazement as a cultivated sense of wonder and awe about aspects of life that are familiar and usually taken for granted. Essentially, if we aspire to regard all of God's creations with amazement, then we might find that we are able to treat even our surliest teenagers with curiosity and admiration.

Curious Prompts

Let's return to the practical aspects of communication. In Chapter 4, I wrote about using reflections to slow down a conversation, learn about your adolescent's perspective, and help them to feel understood. Curious prompts are a complement to reflections that serve a similar function. Here are two all-purpose curious prompts:

Tell me more

Help me understand

Just like with reflections, the tone of your voice should be calm and assertive. You can deploy these in a wide variety of circumstances, and they are an easy alternative to the righting reflex. These prompts are also great training wheels for parents who are having trouble coming up with good reflections.

SOPHIE: I've barely slept this week. There's just way too much going on.
TARA: Huh. Tell me more.

MARK: I'm never gonna find a job in my field . . . Maybe I'll just move to some kind of commune where I can be the nanny or potato peeler or whatever.
DAVID: Sounds groovy. Tell me more.

ROOPA: If I quit social media, I'll have literally no friends.
AARAV: Help me understand why you feel that way.

RYAN: Taking drug tests makes me want to smoke more.
STEPHEN: I don't really get it. Help me understand.

See? No reflection, no problem. Go with a curious prompt.

Curious Questions

We all love to be asked thoughtful questions that convey nonjudgmental interest in our lives and perspectives. Here are some tips for asking great questions.

First, questions should be open-ended whenever possible. An open-ended question cannot be answered in a word, and it has no right or wrong response. It often starts with *what* or *how*, which invite descriptive answers. Second, questions should be curious. They shouldn't be designed to prove a point or lead to a certain conclusion. They should be asked in a spirit of genuine inquiry, with the belief that you don't already know the answer. Third, questions must not be advice in disguise. Don't worry, I *do* want your adolescent to hear and accept your advice (skip ahead to Chapter 7 for more on that). But this isn't the way to do it. Dressed-up advice (*Have you tried telling your teacher how you feel? Why don't you start with an outline? Can you ask your friend for help?*) fails the curiosity test, because it is essentially a righting reflex wearing a false mustache.

An additional note about questions: one curious question is fantastic, but too many questions can feel more like an interrogation than a partnership. Alternate questions with reflections or other speech to avoid this dynamic.

Transforming Questions from Closed to Open

It takes practice to master the art of open-ended questions. The good news is that unlike reflections, which you have to improvise based on what your adolescent says, questions can be planned in advance. So before you approach your child for a hard talk, think about what questions you want to ask, and then revise those until you are confident that your questions are open-ended and curious. Here are some examples of what that transformation looks like:

Did you do your homework?	• What kind of homework do you have? • How will you get it all done?
Are you all packed for our trip?	• What do you still need to do to be ready?
Will there be alcohol at this party?	• What will the party be like? • How do your friends feel about alcohol? • What do you see as the pros and cons of drinking? • How will you get home safely?
You're not having unprotected sex, are you?	• What's your plan for avoiding pregnancy and STDs? • How do you and your boyfriend communicate about those issues?

The answers to these questions will let you know what your adolescent is thinking and whether you may need to intervene with advice, assistance, or direction. If your teen can recite a straightforward list of assignments and communicate a plan for getting the work done, then your best move is simply to get out of the way. This is how you help them to feel understood (you can appreciate their considerable workload), confident (you won't undermine their plan with extraneous advice), and in control (you let them get on with it). Alternatively, if the family is headed to the airport in three hours and your son is vague about what's in his suitcase and whether he's bringing a phone charger and toothbrush, then you know that he may need some assistance. At that point, you can ask further questions—*What clothes are you bringing? What toiletries? How do you plan to entertain yourself on the plane? How will you charge your electronic devices?*—or give instructions to structure the task ahead.

Questions about finishing homework and packing a suitcase are straightforward enough. But if you cringed while reading the questions about substances and sex, you're not alone. It takes some chutzpah to form these words in your mouth and say them out loud to anyone, much less a member of your own family. This is doubly true if you and your child have been participating in the polite charade (far less common these days than when I was a teen) in which parents pretend that they are in control and teens pretend that they are following their parents' explicit rules and implied preferences. Open-ended questions force you to talk to each other instead of avoiding embarrassing or controversial topics with simple yes or no answers. Of course, if you dare to ask your kids open-ended questions, such as *What do think about marijuana? What kind of birth control are you using?* they just might tell you the truth, and you can't get mad at them for answering honestly. So don't ask until you are ready and willing to hear about it.

Jasmine and Khalil

Remember Jasmine and Khalil from Chapter 2? Khalil is a nineteen-year-old dealing with the amorphous loneliness of life after high school. He is living with his mom and working as a coordinator within the oncology department at the hospital in his town, and though the work pays decently and is clearly important (helping cancer patients organize a complex schedule of medications and appointments, and assisting them with their bills), most of his coworkers are twice his age or older. He likes the job, but he isn't sure if it's what he wants to do long-term. His high school friend group has scattered, with some attending college, others working casually for restaurants or ride services, and others (like him) trying to pursue some kind of career path.

Most days after work he watches YouTube and plays video games. He is bored, and maybe just a bit depressed. His mom, Jasmine, hovers around, which he finds annoying. He knows she wants to be helpful, but her offers to cook a meal for him, bring him along while she visits her sisters, or drive him to work are vaguely humiliating. He can sense from three rooms away how nervous she is, and her anxiety feels diminishing; is he so pathetic that his mother has to worry about his mood, social calendar, diet, and whether he'll get to work on time? He just wants to be with people his own age, and that seems to be the exact thing that makes her *most* nervous. He avoids her as much as he can.

It's Friday night, and—somewhat miraculously—Khalil has been invited to a party by a cute young medical assistant he occasionally runs into at the hospital. The party is a few towns over, but she offered to pick him up from his house when she leaves work at seven. Khalil gets home at five thirty and immediately showers, chooses his outfit, and oils his braids. He feels his mother's eyes on him, desperate for information he doesn't feel like sharing.

JASMINE: Hey, you look nice.

KHALIL: Thanks.

JASMINE: Are you going out?

KHALIL: Yeah.

JASMINE: Where to?

KHALIL: Just a thing.

JASMINE: Oh, a thing!

KHALIL: A party.

JASMINE: All right. With your cousins?

KHALIL: No, nobody you know.

JASMINE: I'm not asking for the nuclear codes, Khalil. I'm just curious.

KHALIL: A girl from work invited me. She's gonna pick me up.

JASMINE: Is it far?

KHALIL: I don't know. She invited me, I said sure, and then she said she could give me a ride since we live near the hospital and she's getting off soon.

JASMINE: Will she drive you home? I don't want you to ride with someone who's been drinking.

KHALIL: I don't know. I'll figure it out.

I'll interrupt this lovely exchange here. Jasmine has hit a wall. There are three reasons her questions did not elicit a more reciprocal conversation. One, she has a bad track record of reacting with anxious disapproval when Khalil tells her about his plans, and he doesn't want to deal with that energy right now. To get him to open up, she has to show him that she can hear his answers without anxiety or judgment. Two, her questions were mostly closed-ended. Finally, her questions showed that she is preoccupied with matters of logistics and safety, implying that she doesn't have confidence in Khalil to figure out his own plans and return home safely. She wasn't trying to control him, but he wasn't feeling understood or confident in this conversation.

Of course, from Jasmine's perspective, she was not being overly strict or nosy—just practical and protective. Their town's police department has a reputation for harassing young black men like her son late at night. She wanted to know whether he'd be drinking and where he would be so she could be prepared to give him a ride home or intervene in some other way if necessary. She was also on guard for potential heartbreak. Khalil has not always shown the best judgment when it comes to romance, and when his last girlfriend turned out to be seeing someone else, he got seriously depressed. Of course, Khalil knows his mother well enough to see right through her barrage of questions. He resents being worried about and fussed over; it makes him feel like she doesn't think he's capable of handling himself.

Let's give Jasmine another shot—this time she'll try to be more authentically curious, rather than anxious and expectant, about his plans for the evening. She'll also try to intersperse her questions with other comments so that Khalil doesn't feel like he's being interrogated.

JASMINE: Hey, you look nice.

KHALIL: Thanks.

JASMINE: What are your plans?

KHALIL: A party.

JASMINE: Fun! You look ready.

KHALIL: Yeah, my ride won't be here for a while. I guess I'm just excited.

JASMINE: Come sit with me for a few minutes since you're not in a rush.

KHALIL: Okay.

JASMINE: Who's your ride?

KHALIL: This girl from work.

JASMINE: What's her name?

KHALIL: Alicia. She's a medical assistant.

JASMINE: Alicia the medical assistant. Sounds promising!

KHALIL: I don't know her that well.

JASMINE: I'm just excited for you, that's all.

KHALIL: It's definitely been a while since I made any new friends. I don't want to jinx it.

JASMINE: Understood. What's going on at work lately?

KHALIL: Actually, something pretty interesting happened today. This patient showed me these bills she was getting, and they were just ridiculous. Like the insurance was barely covering any of the treatment. So I did some research, made some phone calls, and I found out that other patients are having this problem too, and it's actually illegal. The insurance company is supposed to be covering it. Most of the patients just pay the bill because they don't want to fall behind, and what are they going to do? It's cancer, they need the treatment. Anyway, long story, but a lot of these people are going to be getting a big check back from the insurance company based on what I found.

JASMINE: What? Honey, that's amazing!

KHALIL: Not gonna lie, it felt good.

JASMINE: You helped a lot of people!

KHALIL: I know! I'm like, damn, I'm good at this.

JASMINE: I'm impressed.

KHALIL: You've been saying that since I was playing with Legos. Anyway, I'm going to run to the store before Alicia gets here. Don't want to show up to a party empty-handed.

JASMINE: Okay. By the way, when do you think you'll be home tonight?

KHALIL: I'm not sure. I'll probably get a car service. Don't worry about me.

JASMINE: Would you really believe me if I said I wouldn't worry? Seriously, if you need a ride, you can always call me. Day or night. I trust you to figure it out though.
KHALIL: I will. Thanks, Mom.
JASMINE: Have fun!

What changed? In this conversation, Jasmine's questions were relaxed, nonjudgmental, and showed true curiosity about Khalil's job and social life. Rather than asking whether his coworker might be drinking (which could be interpreted as judgmental, thus spoiling the rest of the conversation), Jasmine asked about her name. She didn't learn much, but it was more than nothing. She also invited him to share about his job, rather than grilling him on the specifics of his plans for the evening. This gave Khalil the opportunity to tell her a story he felt proud about, and it gave her a chance to openly admire his accomplishment. Jasmine ended the conversation by offering Khalil a ride home, but also saying explicitly that she trusted his judgment. He may or may not accept her offer of a ride, but he won't be rejecting it just to prove that he doesn't need her help.

Hard Talk Highlights

- Rekindling a sense of wonder about teens' inner lives, ambitions, and abilities is an important part of building a partnership as they gain independence.

- Although we know our children intimately, practicing "beginner's mind" helps us to ask good questions and listen earnestly to the answers we hear.

- Getting adolescents to talk about their behavior and inner life requires parents to get curious, set aside their judgment and righting reflex, and manage the anxieties that arise.

- Ask open-ended questions that can't be answered in a word, have no right or wrong response, and aren't designed to prove a point.

- Too many questions can feel more like an interrogation than a partnership. Alternate questions with reflections or other speech to avoid this dynamic.

CHAPTER 6
MOTIVATION FROM WITHIN

Motivation is the *why* of all behavior. Without motivation, we atrophy as human beings. Although some people do suffer from a true lack of motivation, this is most common in patients suffering from serious mental illnesses such as schizophrenia, or those who have experienced a neurological event such as a traumatic brain injury or stroke.

More commonly we berate ourselves or others for being unmotivated when really motivation is complex, not absent. I may *want* to get to the gym, but I am even more motivated to avoid shoveling my car out from a snowbank, which I would need to do before leaving the house. You feel motivated to perfect a spreadsheet before sending it to your boss, until your best friend texts to ask whether you'd like to go out for a drink, and that sounds even more attractive. As I pointed out in Chapter 4, ambivalence—holding two or more conflicting goals—is a normal and healthy aspect of motivation. Our human hearts are complicated; motivation is rarely a straight arrow.

How different people find motivation can be like those pictures that look like a goblet or two faces, a rabbit or a duck. The picture is ambiguous; it contains both images. It's silly to argue about which image is "correct." You want your teen to take a summer class to strengthen her college application; she might be motivated to do it because it's an opportunity to spend time with her best friend. You'd like your young adult to renew his car insurance because (hello) it's illegal to drive without it; he's motivated to prepare for a road trip he's planning with his roommates.

Over and over, I have seen young people and their parents look at the same problem and describe it in different ways. Families can get stuck in conflict and power struggle over whose definition of the problem is more accurate, when the important thing is to pick a solution and move forward. It ultimately doesn't matter whose explanation is correct, so long as the solution is acceptable to everyone.

For example, a parent might describe a problem as *my daughter smokes too much weed*, while the daughter describes the problem as *my mom won't mind her own business*. Although we may instinctively find the mother's view more compelling, the person at the center of the concern in this scenario is the daughter. Her parents need her investment in solving the problem, or nothing will change. Sure, her parents can implement various consequences or rewards to try and shift her position, but if the motivation doesn't come from within, then the contingencies are ultimately superficial, short-term manipulations. She will not be motivated to fix a problem that she doesn't think exists, so any solution must address a problem that she is motivated to work on—for instance, talking with a family therapist about the constant conflict in the home.

When it comes to capitalizing on adolescents' motivation, it's helpful to remember that young people are often more motivated by short-term and socially oriented goals than long-term projections. That's just how their brains work: they are less risk-averse and more reward-sensitive than adults. That doesn't mean they don't have values. They do. But broadly speaking, adolescents tend to value immediate rewards over long-term ones, and social fulfillment over individual achievement.

Adolescence is like a different country. You lived there once, and you might have thought and behaved in ways that are inexplicable to you now. Since we know that adolescence is a temporary address, we tend to devalue its culture and mores. But in this life, we are all just traveling through. The perspective of middle age is simply that—a different perspective. These divergent worldviews result in adults and adolescents talking past each other, stuck at an impasse of misunderstanding. To appeal to the better angels of adolescents' natures, we must take them seriously as moral agents instead of dismissing their perspective as limited or immature.

Internal versus External Motivation

In the world of child psychology, much ink has been devoted to the concepts of internal versus external motivation. External motivation comes from gaining rewards or avoiding consequences; *behaviorism* is a term for using external motivators to shape behavior. Internal motivation comes from within: doing something because you like to. Research has shown that for both adults and children, internal motivation is the more powerful and long-lasting driver of behavior. External reinforcements and consequences can certainly have an immediate and notable impact on behavior—that's why it works so well to occasionally bribe my kids to get into the car by promising snacks once their seat belts are buckled. When external motivation works well, it is like a battery that jump-starts a new behavior, and internal motivation eventually takes over to maintain the change. For example, you might offer some external motivation to a teenager for going to bed before eleven p.m. in the hope that after a week or so of trying this new routine, the teenager will feel so much better that he will be internally motivated to continue prioritizing sleep.

But external motivators don't work well for all kids, and in general they are more effective with younger children than with adolescents. If you have tried and failed to use rewards and punishments to influence your adolescent's behavior, you have experienced firsthand the very real limitations of the behaviorist approach. First, external motivation can fade quickly once the contingencies are removed, so unless you plan on doling out rewards forever, it's not necessarily a long-term solution. Second, people—especially teens—are fantastic at gaming the system. If your adolescent is not internally motivated to comply with your goals, she will probably figure out how to pretend to comply to avoid punishment or reap rewards. Third, research shows that rewards can, horrifyingly, decrease internal motivation and worsen performance. In other words, offering incentives for a given behavior or task can actually interfere with a person's long-term motivation to do it.

But here is the issue that most concerns me: rewards and consequences can undermine adolescents' sense of being understood, confident, and in control, thereby triggering a power struggle and damaging the partnership goal. That's why I advise parents to think critically about the pros and cons of using external motivators (rewards and consequences) as kids get older. Rewards are, at best, a short-term strategy for boosting motivation. And while punishments (consequences) do work for some kids, they backfire so enormously with others that I usually don't recommend them to parents of adolescents.

This is confusing for some people, who assume that no punishment means no rules or expectations. This is not true. Parents can talk clearly and often about rules, just as you might in any healthy relationship. For example, if a friend stood you up for lunch, you would be mad. You could say, "I was upset when you flaked. I expected you to be there." If your spouse spilled food all over the couch and didn't bother to clean it up, you would (I hope) confront them about that violation of house rules. It doesn't naturally follow that you would take away your friend's phone or cancel your partner's weekend plans. You would assume that these people are internally motivated to have a good relationship with you and are therefore able to listen and change when you explain your boundaries and expectations.

In fact, using rewards and punishments to influence kids' behavior is less standard than you might assume. While this approach represents the norm in many cultures, the use of contingencies to motivate children is far from universal. A survey of parents in China, India, Italy, Kenya, the Philippines, and Thailand found that these practices were relatively uncommon. The most common tactics that parents who participated in this survey used to deal with misbehavior were talking with kids about expectations, scolding, and asking the child to repair the situation or apologize. Punishments (hitting, removing privileges, or issuing time-outs) and rewards (promising treats for better behavior) were not unheard of, but they were not universal either.

I asked Dr. David Henderson, my boss at Boston Medical Center and an expert in global psychiatry, for some context. Dr. Henderson has practiced psychiatry on five continents, so he's seen how parents around the world manage conflict and motivation with teens and young adults. He notes that every culture has unspoken expectations about when and whether adolescents make their own decisions versus obey parents' directions, and that even within cultures there is a lot of variation from family to family. In some countries physical punishment (hitting) is common, while in others it is unusual or even illegal. However, expectations about obedience don't always translate to actual compliance. He's seen how even adolescents in cultures with more authoritarian parenting styles crave independence and autonomy.

When it comes to seeking psychiatric or medical care, the United States and Canada are somewhat exceptional regarding concern for the privacy and autonomy of the individual. Dr. Henderson has practiced in settings where not just parents but an entire extended family shows up for a twenty-year-old's psychiatry appointment, and treatment decisions are negotiated between the doctor and the head of the family unit (not the individual with the problem). But the dynamics of internal and external motivation play out just the same. Adolescents may initially agree to try a medication or change their behavior to comply with their parents' (or doctor's) expectations, but if they don't have any internal motivation to maintain the change, compliance tends to be short-lived. He's even seen how expectations of compliance can backfire: for example, at a clinic in Cambodia, patients assured their doctors that they were taking their medicine as prescribed, but their blood work indicated they were hardly taking it at all. When researchers asked the patients why they lied, they said that they didn't want to upset the doctors by admitting that they had reservations about the treatment. Even in a culture where people generally defer to authority figures in public, they followed their internal motivations when they got home.

In order to have meaningful influence, we have to be curious and attuned to whether kids are following our rules and advice. That doesn't mean being tepid or uncertain about our expectations, but rather showing a real desire to understand what's getting in the way of following the rules and why.

Powerful Questions

The skills I want to introduce in this chapter are not entirely new. Instead, I will show you how to tweak the questions and reflections described in Chapters 4 and 5 to emphasize and elicit internal motivation. Often, power struggles become particularly acute when the conflict touches on deeply held values without us quite realizing it. By getting kids to talk about their values and reflecting on our own, we can sometimes reveal the root cause of the power struggle and find solutions that were inaccessible moments before.

Unfortunately, you can't come right out and ask *What value is motivating you right now?* That's far too abstract for most people. While you might be reading this book because you value *being a good parent,* and

I might be writing it because I value *creativity, helping others,* and *advancing my career,* the values activating most day-to-day situations are more ambiguous and harder to pin down. Sometimes our only clue that our values have been violated or threatened is when we find ourselves becoming unexpectedly emotional in the middle of a conversation about something else. Adolescents typically struggle even more than adults to articulate their deep motivations without a little help. That's where powerful questions come in.

Powerful questions are open-ended questions that prompt kids to talk about their values. Here are some powerful questions you can use. The answers to these questions will help illuminate your child's values and goals, which may be different from your own.

> *If you had a magic wand, what would you change about this situation?*
>
> *What is most important to you?*
>
> *What are you most concerned about?*
>
> *Help me understand why this means so much to you.*

Affirmations

A skilled practitioner of motivational interviewing is always listening for values. If I think I spot one, I run in that direction. Like a field scientist studying butterflies, I want to get a good look at the butterfly without harming it through overhandling. I try to help my patients discover their internal motivations and connect those values to their behaviors. I *don't* want to accidentally undermine motivation by trampling that butterfly with my own irrelevant ideas and opinions.

Affirmations are reflections that focus on a person's strengths, skills, values, and deep motivations. A well-placed affirmation is like a gentle butterfly net that enables both you and your child to marvel at your child's abilities and values. Good affirmations will strengthen adolescents' internal motivation and help them feel more confident in their ability to try something new or commit to a change.

Affirmations are different from praise because they center your child's values rather than your own. Praise is about meeting expectations; affirmations are about acknowledging motivation. Sometimes the difference between affirmation and praise is semantic, but overall, adolescents prefer when we appreciate and recognize them on their own terms rather than evaluating them on ours. Here are some examples of parents using affirmations to reflect and amplify their adolescents' motivations.

KHALIL: I probably won't know anyone at the party, but I'm trying to meet people.
JASMINE: You're really putting yourself out there.

RYAN: I don't see what's so bad about marijuana, but I'd be willing to quit if I knew they'd let me back on the football team.
STEPHEN: Football is more important to you than weed.

ROOPA: Everyone acts so fake on Instagram.
PRIYA: Connecting with people on a deeper level is important to you.

SOPHIE: I hate organic chemistry! I'm only taking it because it's required for medical school applications.
TARA: Becoming a doctor is a big motivator.

Affirmations are also helpful when you are trying to find common ground in a conflict. Even if you don't like your teen's behavior, you can affirm the values that they are expressing through their words or actions. Here are some examples:

> I admire your commitment to your friends, but you can't stay over at Alana's house without asking me.

> I hear that you take your faith very seriously and want to have an authentic connection with God. Even as you explore these ideas, I want you to attend your cousin's bar mitzvah as a way of being present for your family.

> You're working so hard and excelling at cheerleading. I'm worried that academics aren't getting enough of your time and attention.

> It's great that you want to take full responsibility for your summer activities. I hope you understand that your choices will have an effect on the whole family's planning, and that you'll talk with us before making any decisions.

Julia and Jack

Jack, fourteen, has type 1 diabetes. For the first few years after his diagnosis, his mom, Julia, supervised his food and insulin carefully. Now that he has started high school, he is spending much more time unsupervised. His blood sugar has been veering into scary numbers, and last week someone from the school called Julia to pick Jack up early because he wasn't feeling well. When she arrived at the school, he was sweaty, shaky—clearly hypoglycemic. Julia is distraught. She wants Jack to have the full, normal life he craves, bouncing from early morning crew practice to a fleet of advanced classes to endless hours of goofing around at friends' houses after school. He has always been such a bright, energetic kid, and she hates to stand in between her son and the world. But it seems like Jack can't handle the responsibility of managing his illness on his own. He just isn't taking it seriously.

Julia knows that if Jack fails to manage his illness properly, he is at risk for serious and terrifying complications: nerve damage, blindness, kidney disease. After the incident at school last week, she really spelled it all out for him and emphasized that he could harm his body irreparably or even die. She warned him that if he couldn't manage his diet and insulin in the mornings, then he would have to quit rowing or even take some time off school to get things under control. In the moment, she felt like she had really gotten through to him. But today, again, the school nurse called midday to say that Jack seemed ill. When Julia rushes into the nurse's office with juice and candy, Jack sighs and lifts his shirt so she can fiddle with the settings on his insulin pump until she is satisfied. Twenty minutes later, they are sitting in the car outside of the building, and Julia is fuming.

JULIA: I don't get it. You know that you could become seriously ill if you don't get on top of this.

JACK: Yeah, I know. Whatever.

JULIE: No, not whatever! This is not whatever at all. I can't believe we are having this conversation again.

JACK: Okay, okay, sorry.

JULIA: Why are you apologizing to me? You're only hurting yourself. I hate to say this, but I'm not sure crew is such a good idea this year. You're just a freshman. Maybe you're not ready to be on your own in the mornings.

JACK: Mom! You are overreacting. I'll be fine.

JULIA: It's! Not! Fine!

Julia realizes that she is about to cry. She takes a deep breath.

JULIA: I'm sorry . . . can we start this conversation over? Help me understand. What's been getting in the way of checking your sugars and counting carbs?

JACK: Well, here's the thing. Crew practice starts at six thirty, so Cameron and Josh pick me up at six. I always bring something to eat in the car, like a banana or whatever. And once we start practice, I'm really careful to make sure my pump doesn't get wet. It's kind of a joke—the other guys are always apologizing if I get splashed or whatever.

JULIA: Are those boys bullying you?

JACK: No! No, Mom, it's not like that. They're my friends. It's just—you just wouldn't understand.

JULIA: Okay, okay, sorry. It is hard for me to understand. But you were saying, you eat in the car, and then you're very careful to make sure your pump doesn't get wet.

JACK: Yeah, exactly. So we practice on the water for an hour, then change as fast as we can in the locker rooms. There is no time to eat or buy a drink or anything. I don't like people staring at my pump, so I don't mess with it when I'm around my friends, and I silence the glucose monitor so people won't stare at me if I start beeping.

JULIA: Wow . . . stressful.

JACK: It's just, I'm in such a rush. And there's no privacy in the locker room.

JULIA: If you had a few more minutes and a private space, you could adjust your insulin and have a snack.

JACK: Yeah, I guess so.

JULIA: Can I ask you another question? Aren't you worried about all the terrible potential medical complications of diabetes? Losing your eyesight? Having a stroke?

JACK: Honestly, I don't think about that stuff.

JULIA: You're not worried about that.

JACK: Nah, that won't happen to me.

JULIA: Hmm. Well, what is most important to you?

JACK: Well, for one, I'd like to avoid my mom sprinting into school with juice boxes and lifting up my shirt— that's pretty embarrassing. Missing class is not great. And I really, really want to keep rowing. Please don't make me quit.

JULIA: It sounds like you value being self-sufficient. You don't like me babying you, and you want to do well in school and crew. And when you don't have the time and space to manage your insulin, all of that falls apart and I come running through the hall like a madwoman. Am I getting that right?

JACK: Ha, yeah, basically.

JULIA: So Mr. Self-Sufficient, how do you want to fix this problem?

JACK: I guess I need some time and a private space between practice and homeroom. And food.

JULIA: Could you leave practice a few minutes early?

JACK: I guess . . . but I really don't want to. Putting the boats away is a lot of work, and it would feel bad to not help. Then we ride to school, and I rush to homeroom. It's crazy, I'm racing just to get there and sit around. Nothing even happens in homeroom, just announcements and attendance and stuff. I'd rather skip that.

JULIA: How feasible is that?

JACK: Uh, I'm not sure. What if I kept a stash of snacks in Nurse Chris's office and went there instead of straight to homeroom? That way I have a private place to do my thing. I would be a few minutes late to homeroom, but Nurse Chris could explain the situation to Ms. Schwartz.

JULIA: I like that idea. Very responsible.

JACK: We're still sitting here. Can we go back inside and ask her?

JULIA: Sure, let's do it. I do have one additional request though.

JACK: What?

JULIA: I don't like you silencing the alarm on your glucose monitor. It's there for a reason. If you can keep your sugar in a good place, it won't go off. Can you please promise me you'll keep the alarm on?

JACK: Yeah, okay. I promise.

JULIA: Awesome. Let's go back in and talk to Nurse Chris.

In this hard talk, Julia realized that she and Jack had different motivations, but that was okay. Once Julia stopped focusing on her own motivation—fear of medical complications—she could appreciate Jack's own motivation and work with that. Jack's lack of concern about long-term health consequences baffled Julia, but it just wasn't productive to keep having that argument. By accepting this and turning the conversation toward what was most important to him, Julia was able to elicit Jack's reasons for controlling his blood sugar.

Julia's greatest fear, that Jack was not motivated to manage his illness properly, turned out not to be true. But she had to listen carefully and nonjudgmentally to understand and affirm Jack's own values and motivations: excelling in athletics and in school, proving he could be self-sufficient, and fitting in with his new friends. Julia skillfully pointed out that properly attending to his diabetes would enable Jack to achieve those goals and that hypoglycemic crises are not compatible with athletic performance *or* fitting in. It was a tremendous relief to Julia to hear that Jack did in fact have powerful motives for wanting to control his diabetes, and Jack was also relieved that his mom could recognize his reasons as valid.

Despite their overall agreement on a plan for addressing Jack's recurring low blood sugar, Julia did make an additional, specific request at the end of this conversation. You may have noticed that this is a recurring theme in the hard talks. Julia asked Jack to stop silencing his glucose monitor; Jasmine reminded Khalil to call if he needed a ride; David suggested that Mark get a haircut.

Parents really do have important information and advice to share. In the next chapter, I'll finally tackle how to give that advice so that adolescents will be able to hear it and be willing to follow it.

Hard Talk Highlights

- Ambivalence—holding two or more conflicting goals at the same time—is a normal and healthy aspect of motivation.

- Young people are often more motivated by short-term and socially oriented goals than long-term projections. That's just how their brains work: they are less risk-averse and more reward-sensitive than adults.

- To appeal to the better angels of adolescents' natures, we must take them seriously as moral agents instead of dismissing their perspective as limited or immature.

- Powerful questions are open-ended questions that prompt kids to talk about their values.

- Affirmations are reflections that focus on a person's strengths, skills, values, and deep motivations. Affirmations are different from praise because they center your child's values rather than your own.

CHAPTER 7

FINDING SOLUTIONS

The goal of motivational interviewing is usually behavior change. You might have picked up this book because you are hoping to see a change in your child's behavior: you'd like him to finish his homework, answer texts, drive responsibly, or stay away from drugs and alcohol. And yet, you have read six full chapters about active listening and competing theories of motivation. You are a patient person. Or maybe not! If you skipped to this chapter, hoping to get straight to the main course, welcome. That's fine. You and I have a lot in common. I recommend that at some point you review the information in the prior chapters, but of course I can't make you.

This chapter is about making the shift from listening to problem-solving, from venting about or analyzing a dilemma to doing something to change it. The goal is to help your child to get motivated and ready to try something new. This chapter will also cover the role of advice: how to give it, and when to hold back.

Solution-Focused Questions

Although taking the time to listen to and understand your child's dilemma is the foundation of the hard talks approach, I don't want you to get stuck in "analysis paralysis." That's what happens when we get so bogged down by the details of our problems that we never get around to solving them. You might know what this feels like: obsessing over what every person in an interaction said and what they meant, recalling all the twists and turns in how a situation came to be, or getting stuck in the yeah-buts, where every idea is met with *yeah, but.*

Figuring out when to turn the corner from venting toward problem-solving can be a tricky business, and I haven't figured out an exact formula for it. But you don't have to hear every detail of who is and isn't invited to the prom after-party to understand the gist of your teen's dilemma and how she feels about it. Once you feel that you've more or less got it and your kid has had a chance to explain her view, you can prompt her to start thinking about solutions. While some teens naturally want to solve problems, others can get stuck in cycles of rumination and need some help getting off that mental treadmill.

When you sense the time is right, nudge the conversation into problem-solving mode by asking a solution-focused question. Solution-focused questions are open-ended questions that get your child thinking about how to address her dilemma. If this is a problem she has been dealing with for a long time (e.g., a difficult peer who has been in her class since kindergarten), you can acknowledge her past efforts to deal with the problem by asking, *What have you already tried?* and *How did that go?* If the problem is new, or if she is ready to consider her next steps, your questions can focus on the future. Some great solution-focused questions are:

What could you do?

What solutions do you have in mind?

How do you want to handle this?

Not all your adolescent's solutions will be gems. Encourage her to consider the pros and cons of each idea. Sure, you *could* uninvite someone from the party: *How would that go? What are the pros and cons of doing that?* By guiding through questions rather than shooting down bad ideas, you can stay in partnership mode rather than giving into a righting reflex.

Don't leave any solutions off the table. *Do nothing and accept the situation as it is* can be a good solution. Considering one's options and consciously deciding on acceptance as a strategy can be very empowering. Not every problem can be solved. Talking to an adult with a sympathetic ear and weighing the pros and cons of different approaches can help adolescents feel much better about situations they cannot change.

At some point in the conversation, it may become glaringly obvious that your child is missing some key information or doesn't have the life experience to come up with a good idea about how to proceed. She might not know that the party is bound to be so large that she can avoid the problematic peer fairly easily, or she might be comforted by the funny story of how you accidentally invited your cousin's current and ex-boyfriends to your wedding, and they both showed up! This is when it's appropriate to step in and offer some wisdom. If you have resisted giving advice until this point in the conversation, your patience will be rewarded.

Advice

I don't mean to suggest that advice is taboo. Good advice—especially when it comes from someone who appreciates your dilemma, cares about your well-being, and possesses true expertise—is a rare treasure. As adults, we're on our own so much of the time. We have to google things like "how do you replace car key batteries," "when do I file my taxes," and "suspicious mole." In these contexts, advice from people who know what they are talking about and make the time to explain things saves us money and heartache. It helps us feel less alone in the world and reminds us that we all have people rooting for our success.

But adolescents have the opposite problem: they are inundated by a constant stream of advice, directions, and dire warnings. Just this morning, millions of teens received well-intentioned advice about which jacket to wear, what food to eat, where to sit, and how to succeed in school and life. By the time their history teachers started offering opinions on why adolescents should spend less time playing video games, the "advice" started to sound suspiciously like criticism. And so, for the sake of their collective sanity, they tuned it out.

Consider this: the ability to ignore advice can be a strength rather than a flaw. We all need to sift through the myriad expectations of the people around us and decide for ourselves which path to pursue. Your adolescent might get a lot of terrible advice from both adults and peers on any particular day: *apply to thirty colleges*; *do three hundred push-ups every day*; *text me a nude photo*; *don't tell your parents*. Compared to kids, adults have more experience with disappointing people by ignoring their advice and bucking expectations. Even so, many grown-ups find it difficult or even painful to let down others by not following their advice, even when we have good reasons for doing so. A young person who brushes off advice, scrutinizes it for accuracy, or interrogates the motives of its source may be doing the hard work of critical thinking and establishing healthy boundaries.

So rather than feeling exasperated that your child seems to ignore your instructions, ask yourself, *Under what circumstances would I want my kid to accept anyone's advice?* First, the advice-giver should have the necessary expertise about the issue at hand as well as a solid grasp of your child's specific situation. Applying to thirty colleges might make sense for some seniors, but if yours has guaranteed tuition at a local university, applying beyond that list of schools could be foolish. Second, advice should empower your child, not diminish her.

For example, you hope that your child would follow a race training schedule because she believes the plan will help her get stronger and faster, not because she would be seen as overweight and lazy if she were to disregard it. Finally, your child should know to push back against people who are overly controlling and secretive. You don't want him following the advice of anyone who makes him feel like he's not allowed to say no or talk about the issue with a friend or family member. Those are the tactics of sexual, spiritual, and financial predators. If someone is judgmental and incurious toward your child, belittles them, pressures them, or treats them as anything but an individual worthy of respect, I hope that they will recognize that person's advice as deeply suspect and ignore it.

In other words, we hope that our kids accept advice only from people who make them feel understood, confident, and in control. Oh! So now you get it: "people" includes *you*. When you ensure that your child is feeling understood, confident, and in control before you offer your advice, you maximize the odds that your advice will be heard and considered. You also serve as a model for how other adults should communicate.

So: you're ready. You know that feeling judged, pushed, and inadequate are paralyzing, not motivating. You have all the building blocks—reflections, questions, affirmations, advice—at your disposal. You're practiced using each skill. Turn the page for a step-by-step guide to putting these skills together so that you feel confident having hard talks with your almost-grown-up kids.

Putting It Together:
A Five-Step Guide to Hard Talks

1 SET THE STAGE

Think about when, where, and how you want to initiate a potentially sensitive conversation. When is a good time? Try to start your talk at a time when you and your adolescent are both feeling relaxed and have some time to chat. It's not great to bring up your concerns when your kid is on the way out the door, other people are watching, or you're already fighting about something else.

Where do you want to talk? Consider saving a hard talk for a walk or drive; movement seems to lower anxiety and help people get unstuck. Talking while walking or driving also cuts way down on eye contact, decreasing the overall intensity of the interaction. In my experience, too much eye contact can make an uncomfortable conversation feel unbearable.

How do you start the conversation? Be direct, brief, and concrete. Voice an observation that is a fact, not an opinion. For example, if you have concerns about a teen's hygiene, you could say, *I noticed that you haven't showered in a few days.*

2 ASK QUESTIONS

Give your child a chance to respond to your observation. It's okay to sit (or walk) in silence for a minute or two. If your observation alone isn't generating a lot of conversation or your adolescent seems defensive, ask some open-ended, curious questions. You could say, *What's behind that change?* or *What's getting in the way?* The great thing about questions is you can think of them ahead of time, so have a few good ones ready to go.

3 REFLECT WORDS AND FEELINGS

No matter what your kid says next, commit to reflection. Pause after a reflection, listen carefully, and let your child know you're listening by offering substantive reflections. Make sure your voice is calm and neutral. Look for opportunities to affirm values and motivation. Save any advice, opinions, and personal experiences for later in the conversation. Keep your child and his perspective in the spotlight. Continue listening, reflecting, and asking questions for longer than you feel is necessary.

4 LOOK FOR SOLUTIONS

Once you have a solid understanding of your child's dilemma and perspective, gently turn the conversation toward solutions by asking a solution-focused question such as, *What do you think would help?* Listen to his ideas. If he generates good solutions, encourage him to pursue one or two of those ideas; the solution does not need to come from you. If no good ideas are emerging, proceed to step five.

5 ASK PERMISSION TO GIVE ADVICE

Always ask before you give advice. You could say, *Can I make a suggestion?* or *I went through something similar; can I tell you about it?* If you have done the work of listening without judgment, your child should say yes. Give your advice. A little goes a long way, so don't unload your fourteen-point plan all at once. You could say, *You could set an alarm on your phone for nine p.m. that would remind you to take a shower before it's so late that you're too tired to do it.* Then ask for feedback: *What do you think about that?* Don't be offended if your advice isn't immediately embraced; sometimes kids need a little time to commit to a plan of action.

That's it! Your child now knows that you have your eye on this issue and that he can talk to you about it without triggering an argument, criticism, or unsolicited advice. He has a good idea of a solution to pursue. You may have some role in implementing that solution, or not. Now it is time to change the subject. Don't undo your great work by belaboring the issue and being too pushy. Switch to a lighter, uncontroversial topic—sports, TV, an upcoming event—and check back in about the subject of this hard talk another day. When you do check back in, start the five steps all over again: make an observation (e.g., *The other day we talked about using an alarm as a shower reminder*) and ask a question (e.g., *How has that been working out?*).

My favorite aspect of the hard talks approach is that it can be used to address literally any concern. Rather than a script, it's a mindset: lead with curiosity and listen more than you speak. Empower the people around you to make great decisions by helping them feel understood, confident, and in control. Let's see an example of how one stepdad uses the approach to help his stepdaughter find solutions in a situation where she feels stuck.

Antonio and Anna

Remember Anna from Chapter 2, the fifteen-year-old who lives with her mom (Carolina) and stepdad (Antonio)? It's now March, and Anna and Carolina are fighting about the family's plans for the Easter holiday and school vacation. Carolina just bought plane tickets for the whole family to spend the week visiting her parents in Florida. Anna is enrolled in several advanced courses and also has a major part in the school's spring play. She was planning to spend the week studying, rehearsing, and hanging out with friends. She also doesn't like going to her grandparents' house because she finds her grandmother overly critical, especially of her weight (too heavy) and her Spanish (not great). Carolina considers the plan a done deal and said as much to Anna last night. A big fight ensued, and when Anna came home from school today, she went straight into her room and hasn't come out since. Antonio hates to get in the middle of his wife and her daughter, who are both terrifyingly smart and stubborn. But he knows that someone has to talk with Anna. He knocks on her door.

ANNA: What?
ANTONIO: Hey, will you come shopping with me?
ANNA: Why?
ANTONIO: I want to talk to you about Easter, and I have to go to the store to get snacks for your little brother's class for tomorrow. Just walk down the block with me. I don't want to carry all those juice boxes back myself. Please?
ANNA: Fine.
She emerges from her room, and they begin walking down the street.
ANTONIO: So. You don't want to go to Florida for the holiday.
ANNA: I already talked about it with Mom.

ANTONIO: Yes, I heard some of that. The whole neighborhood heard. But I don't think I truly understand. What are your concerns?

ANNA: I'm just busy with midterms and the play. I made plans to study and rehearse with people that week. You guys never asked if I already had plans. I guess what I want just doesn't matter.

ANTONIO: You are busy. You work really hard.

ANNA: Plus, I just don't want to be in Miami for that long.

ANTONIO: Why is that?

ANNA: I don't know.

ANTONIO: You don't like your grandparents' house?

ANNA: I don't like being there all week. I have to share a room with Mateo, there is nowhere quiet to be at all, and Abuela thinks I'm too fat. I can see her watching me any time I eat. And I'm even fatter now than last time she saw me.

ANTONIO: You feel like she is judging your weight.

ANNA: I know she is! I heard her say something to Mom about it. She thinks I don't understand Spanish, but I do.

ANTONIO: I'm sorry, Anna. That must have been very painful.

ANNA: It's not your fault. I just don't want to be there for a whole week. A day or two, fine, but don't subject me to a whole week.

ANTONIO: What makes the shorter visits easier for you?

ANNA: Oh, I can deal with anyone for a few hours at a time. It's just, a week . . . I don't know.

ANTONIO: So a few hours at a time with your abuela is no problem.

ANNA: Of course not. She's sweet, in her way. And I know it's important to Mom.

ANTONIO: But a week feels like a long time. What would make the visit more enjoyable for you?

ANNA: I really need some quiet time to study.

ANTONIO: I understand that. Doing well on your exams is really important to you. Where could you study during the trip?

ANNA: Well, could you drive me to the library near her house in the mornings? Just for a few hours?

ANTONIO: Sure, I would do that. That's a good idea. What else?

ANNA: I mean, Mateo gets bored too—he starts climbing the walls, knocking over all the little Jesus figurines and getting on everyone's nerves. Could we get out of the house every afternoon—like take him to the zoo and the playground and whatever?

ANTONIO: That would help you and your brother. I like it.

ANNA: But we really have to do it. You can't forget or change your mind. Mom will feel bad if we're not spending every minute with Abuela.

ANTONIO: Hmm. Can I make a suggestion?

ANNA: Sure, what?

ANTONIO: While you're making all these plans for things you want to do by yourself or with your brother during our visit, can you also make plans for a special activity with your grandmother? That way she won't feel left out.

ANNA: Yeah, that makes sense. Maybe we can bake something or play cards.

ANTONIO: Exactly. Just think about it. So how do you feel about the trip now that we've talked?

ANNA: I'm still kind of mad that Mom didn't tell me before she bought the tickets, but it will be fine.

ANTONIO: Good. So there are twenty kids in Mateo's class—do you think this box of crackers is enough?

ANNA: You better get two.

ANTONIO: Yeah, you're right. The teachers might be hungry too. Hey, can I ask one more thing?

ANNA: What?

ANTONIO: How would you feel if me or your mom spoke with Abuela about the weight thing? I don't want her making you feel bad.

ANNA: Oh no, that would be so embarrassing. Please don't do that. I'd rather handle her myself.

ANTONIO: Sure, sure, I understand.

Antonio moved through each of the five steps in this conversation. He set the stage by inviting Anna on a walk and making a direct, nonjudgmental observation (*you don't want to go to Florida*). He reflected Anna's words and feelings. He asked probing, interested questions. He encouraged her to think of solutions that would make the trip more enjoyable. He gave a bit of advice, after receiving permission to do so. He respected the solution that Anna proposed (making plans to get out of the house) and allowed her to veto his own idea (confronting grandma directly about her focus on Anna's weight).

How Long Should a Hard Talk Last?

A good talk about an important topic might last somewhere between one and one hundred minutes—there's no magic number that's correct. A really great conversation about a topic that neither of you enjoys may involve you asking one question (*What kind of birth control are you using?*), your teenager answering it (*condoms and the pill*), and then you both go on your way (*got it, thanks for letting me know*). If your kid has a great plan and you trust her to follow through on it, you don't need to meddle.

Sometimes parents feel like they are failing at using the motivational interviewing skills because interactions with their kids never continue past five minutes or so. That's okay! As we established in Chapter 2, you are neither friend nor therapist. This is the biggest departure from traditional (therapist-facilitated) motivational interviewing. When a patient talks with a therapist, the therapist gets the patient's undivided attention for fifty minutes. When you use these skills with your adolescent, you are finding opportunities to inject a quick reflection or open-ended question into organic interactions. On the rarer occasions that you intentionally initiate a hard talk, you can use the five steps and draw on all of the skills at once to make sure it goes well, but it's unusual that a young person would have a sustained conversation about anything with their parents for more than ten minutes.

Instead of focusing on the length of your conversations, be honest with yourself about what things have been like in your home. What would constitute a meaningful change? And when change does happen, savor it. Many parents describe what sounds to me like a positive change in their communication with their kids, but they are so hungry for a "perfect" relationship that they dismiss or devalue the progress they are making. For example, if a teen who barely acknowledged you is now agreeing to weekly walks around a local reservoir, don't bemoan the fact that he still goes straight to his room and closes the door after school. The progress is real, and it will annoy your teen if you measure him (and yourself) against an idealized expectation.

But alas, sometimes you will annoy your teen, and sometimes they will annoy you. Like catching colds and running out of milk, irritation is an inevitable part of family life. Read on for some ideas about how to tolerate conflict and recover from it.

Hard Talk Highlights

- While some teens naturally want to solve problems, others can get stuck in cycles of rumination and need some help getting unstuck.

- Solution-focused questions are open-ended questions that get children thinking about how to address their dilemma.

- If your child can't think of a good solution, or is missing important information, it's appropriate to step in and offer some wisdom. If you have resisted giving advice until this point in the conversation, your patience will be rewarded.

- The hard talks approach can be used to address literally any concern. Rather than a script, it's a mindset: lead with curiosity, and listen more than you speak.

- A successful conversation about an important topic might last somewhere between one and one hundred minutes—there's no magic number that's correct.

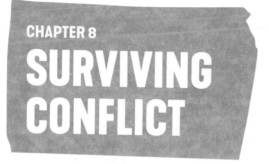

CHAPTER 8

SURVIVING CONFLICT

Although most of us recognize that no relationship is free from conflict, it's hard to remember that when you're in the thick of it. Conflict can feel catastrophic, especially when you feel stuck in disagreement. It's natural to blame ourselves or our kids rather than accepting that arguments and hurt feelings are often unavoidable. We all have our natural ways of expressing frustration with the people we love. In clinic I see a lot of parents who channel that frustration into yelling and crying. I also see parents who intellectualize their conflicts by lecturing and debating. I see families who lose control of their rage and frighten one another with threats or incidents of violence, as well as families who can't stomach conflict at all and choose to avoid people or topics for days, weeks, or even years.

The truth is that arguing with your kids is normal. All relationships involve conflict, so unless you want to live in a cabin in the woods by yourself, you will occasionally find yourself staring unhappily at the people around you. Adolescents are doing the hard work of emotionally separating from parents and preparing for independence. Part of what helps them feel ready to fly is realizing that the nest is . . . kind of annoying. Remembering that adolescents must individuate, that happy families sometimes fight, and that you have the tools you need to work through difficult moments can keep things in perspective.

Maybe you let your righting reflex get the best of you, or your kid was in a foul mood and acted like a jerk, or you were both hungry and stressed. Maybe the topic is so raw and challenging (money, death, etc.) that no human being could handle it perfectly. Maybe you were hoping that for once in their life, your kid would just listen to you, and you wouldn't have to go through a whole five-step process to get them to do the right thing. Adolescents will lie to your face and roll their eyes at your requests, while freely spending your money and trashing your car. When these things happen, getting mad is a fine reaction. It's okay to be human. You are not made of glass and eggshells, and neither is your child. You are both more resilient than that. If you have skills to recover graciously, then these fights will be mere footnotes in the book of your relationship, rather than whole chapters.

Unlike airline representatives or people grabbing the last cart at the supermarket, you will have to deal with your kids for the foreseeable future, so you can't seethe about how you were right and they were wrong forever. Eventually you must dust yourself off and return to the issue that caused the upset. I hope that this chapter offers a few useful strategies for recovering from conflict in a mature, assertive way that you can feel good about (or at least not deeply ashamed of).

This is the only part of the book that is not about motivational interviewing. Therapists don't (or at least, shouldn't!) have intense interpersonal conflicts with their patients, so conflict resolution is less vital in clinical practice. These strategies are ones that I've learned from colleagues and developed in my own practice, and they are consistent with the MI approach.

Take a Break

Most of us know and understand the adage *never go to bed mad.* There is a lot to be said for resolving conflict quickly. However, other people in your household may not share your sense of urgency, and trying to force resolution on someone who is still fuming usually doesn't work out. Taking a break from talking is okay and doesn't mean that you're avoiding conflict or giving up. Allow both yourself and your child an hour (or a day) to reset separately before returning to an issue that you know is fraught.

Watch Your Ratio

One of the best ways to manage the ebb and flow of conflict in family relationships is to attend to the ratio of positive to tense interactions. Psychologist

John Gottman first described this concept in the context of romantic relationship research. Gottman invited married couples to his laboratory, recorded them while they discussed a difficult topic, and then followed up with his research subjects for nine years. He found that the ratio of positive to negative micro-interactions predicted with astonishing accuracy which couples would stay together and which would separate. The "magic ratio" was five to one. In other words, when successful couples talked about difficult subjects, they did make negative and critical statements. But they sprinkled in other types of speech throughout the conversation. Positive interactions don't have to be heart-meltingly sweet. They could be as simple as an attentive *uh huh*, a neutral reflection, or a clarifying question.

Similarly, it is important to make sure that most of your interactions with your child are *not* hard talks. Make time to talk with adolescents about uncontroversial subjects like movies, pets, and food. Better yet, choose some activities that you can do together without talking much at all, like video games, cards, exercise, caring for animals, hiking, and listening to music. Not all bonding requires verbal communication; it can be a relief to spend time together without any pressure to speak. Just getting outside together for a few minutes on a nice day to run an errand or sit on the stoop can be restorative.

A similar concept shows up in the treatment of behavior problems in preschool and elementary school children, when psychologists encourage parents to use a strategy called time-in. A time-in is the opposite of a time-out. It involves spending low-pressure time focused on whatever your child wants to do—in younger children, this might be playing pretend, watching a movie, or coloring. The main rule is that you give your child your full attention and refrain from giving any directions or making any critical comments. Even a little bit of time-in—five minutes for young children, or fifteen minutes for older ones—helps to restore strained relationships. Time-in serves as credit in the bank of your relationship, providing a much-needed cushion against inevitable future withdrawals.

Hand Over Control

Making peace with the fact that you can't control your adolescent's decisions is clearly a theme of this book. Sometimes it can help to acknowledge this explicitly during or after a conflict. If an adolescent is getting upset or annoyed at your expectations, or you feel stuck in a power struggle, you can remind him that ultimately, he is in control. This can feel a little risky, but when it works, it helps restore partnership and reminds an adolescent to take responsibility for his own behavior. When you're attempting a control handover, there is no room for sarcasm. Total earnestness is required to pull this off. Here are some examples.

AARAV: I want you to come straight home after school this week.

ROOPA: You're trying to punish me because some crazy person on the internet saw my account! You have no idea what you're talking about.

AARAV: Okay, okay. I'll be at work, so I can't control what you do after school. I hope you come straight home, but you will need to decide what feels safe while we're working to figure out who sent you those messages.

JASMINE: Here, drive my car to the party.

KHALIL: Stop worrying. I told you, I'm getting a ride.

JASMINE: It sounds like you've made up your mind. I just want to make sure you have a plan for getting home.

TARA: You stay up all hours and then complain about how hard it is to get to class. I don't know why you don't see the connection.

SOPHIE: Stop telling me what to do!

TARA: It's true, I can't make you go to bed; you're too old for that.

Apologize

Our culture is full of people who never apologize, from lying politicians to corporate raiders to rude customers who yell at waiters and clerks. It is important to know that there is no shame, and in fact much grace, to be found in apologizing. It's okay to clear the air with your adolescent by acknowledging your contribution to the conflict and saying that you're sorry. In doing so, you set an important precedent: when we screw up in this world, we apologize. You also lower defenses and set the scene for a mature conversation. Was it cool for your eighteen-year-old to take your car for the evening without asking? No. Was it good form for you to scream that he has the judgment of a kindergartener? Alas, no. You can even go a step further and tell him what you wish you had done differently, as in, *I'm sorry I yelled and said some impulsive things. I wish I had thought to tell you ahead of time that I needed the car last night.*

An important element of an effective apology is that it addresses your behavior and yours alone. If you pivot to highlighting someone else's behavior mid-apology, then the other party is likely to continue defending their actions rather than offering responsibility for their role. *I wish I had thought to tell you ahead of time that I needed the car—but you should never have assumed it was yours to take* invites an argument about reasonable assumptions. When you own your (perhaps minimal) contribution, you encourage others to own theirs. (I'll briefly note here that I am personally terrible at this.)

Be Vulnerable

If your adolescent walked into the room right now, would you hide this book? If the answer is yes, it's worth asking yourself why. Maybe you feel embarrassed about looking for parenting advice. Maybe you want your family to think you've got everything under control. Maybe you're ashamed that you're not 100 percent happy with your relationship with your child. Social work researcher Brené Brown has found that people who are able to describe their vulnerabilities (e.g., *I feel like I should know how to manage conflict with my teen, and I don't*) are more resilient and less trapped by feelings of shame when they fall short. In Brown's words, "vulnerability is a strength rather than a weakness."

Of course, adolescents are super-attuned to their parents' limitations: they already know you're not perfect. If you admit vulnerability to your teenage daughter, she may be disarmed to know that you value her so much that you are seeking out new ideas for understanding her perspective and improving the relationship. It might help her to feel loved and valued. Acknowledging that you sometimes struggle with parenting, and that you are trying out new strategies, is a way of making yourself vulnerable in the service of building partnership. It can also be a good way to respond to potential accusations that you're being "fake" or "weird" as you try out the reflections and other hard talks strategies you've learned in this book. Here are some examples for how that might sound.

JACK: Stop hovering.
JULIA: You feel like I'm hovering.
JACK: I can see you tracking everything I eat.
JULIA: You feel like I'm, uh, tracking everything you eat.
JACK: What? Why are you repeating everything I say?

JULIA: Sorry, I am trying this communication thing I read about, but I'm not very good at it. I'm basically just trying to listen better. Go on.

JACK: Oh, okay . . . whatever. Anyway, your obsessing over my diet is making me really self-conscious. Please stop doing that.

JULIA: I hear you. I'll try.

ANNA: Can you talk to my mom? She says I can't go out this weekend, and she's being totally unfair.

ANTONIO: I don't want to get in the middle of that. Talk to her yourself.

ANNA: You're so inconsistent! Sometimes you're all like, oh what's wrong, how can I help you? And then other times you're like, nope, not getting involved, good luck.

ANTONIO: Hey, I'm doing my best. I don't always know the right thing to say. There's no stepdad instruction manual.

ANNA: I know.

Using the hard talks approach won't prevent every conflict. And sometimes our strong emotions get the better of us. Personally, I am quite familiar with the temptation of giving into anger and just letting people have it. I have been in arguments with my husband and heard the little angel and devil on my shoulders, with the angel whispering, *Ask him why he feels that way* and the devil yelling, *Tell him he's an idiot!* I apologize a lot. But I know that my family is strong enough to withstand a fight every now and then, and so is yours.

Possessing the certainty that this, too, shall pass is a great comfort, and gives us courage to apologize, amend, and try again.

Most of the examples in this book have focused on problems of everyday living: household misunderstandings, academic challenges, and social stress. But as I mentioned in Chapter 1, my clinical specialty is treating serious mental illness. People are usually surprised to realize that no clear line separates mental illness from everyday problems and that the strategies that work to communicate with healthy people encountering stressful situations are also effective in the context of serious mental illness. There are times when people experiencing mental health challenges are too confused or overwhelmed to have a hard talk, but even serious symptoms such as hallucinations and suicidal thoughts tend to ebb and flow, leaving open some windows for meaningful connection. In the next chapter, I'll describe how the hard talks method can be used to encourage a person experiencing mental illness to seek psychiatric treatment.

Hard Talk Highlights

- Remembering that adolescents must individuate, that happy families sometimes fight, and that you have the tools you need to work through difficult moments can keep things in perspective.

- Taking a break from talking is okay and doesn't mean that you're avoiding conflict or giving up.

- Make time for nonverbal activities and conversations about uncontroversial subjects like movies, pets, and food.

- If an adolescent is getting upset or annoyed at your expectations, or you feel stuck in a power struggle, you can remind him that ultimately, he is in control.

- There is no shame, and in fact much grace, to be found in apologizing. The ability to be vulnerable is a strength.

CHAPTER 9
WHEN KIDS STRUGGLE

Do you want to know the big secret about serious mental illness, the number one thing that parenting "experts" and "gurus" won't tell you? Are you ready? Okay, here you go: It. Can. Happen. To. Anyone. The most patient, present, organized, and authoritative parent in the world cannot prevent illnesses like depression, bipolar disorder, schizophrenia, eating disorders, or anxiety from taking hold of their child. Next time you read about a young person experiencing delusions, attempting suicide, or being committed involuntarily to a psychiatric treatment facility, I don't want you to think, *I read parenting books; I attend teacher conferences; that would never happen to my kid.* I want you to think, *There but for the grace of God go I.*

I don't write that to scare you, though the fact of it is terrifying. I write it because there are legions of experts—many of whom believe in their own bullshit!— who promise that if you follow their program, buy their book, or pay for their advice, then your child will grow up to be hardworking, empathetic, intelligent, thin, and especially, especially, especially *not mentally ill.*

I understand how seductive these claims are, but they are 99 percent fiction. Though there is exciting research suggesting that preventing some major mental illness may be possible, these solutions are mostly not in the realm of individual parenting approaches. Promising strategies include reducing fetal exposure to environmental toxins, drugs, and alcohol during pregnancy; preventing obstetric complications and premature birth; addressing the factors that lead to child abuse and neglect; ensuring that young children who experience anxiety and social skill deficits receive timely evidence-based intervention; and implementing legal policies that keep addictive and mind-altering substances away from developing brains.

I can't control my children's personalities or whether they experience mental illness, and neither can you. That may be upsetting to contemplate. But the opposing belief—the theory that you can and should prevent mental illness in your children—is impossible and leads to unnecessary judgment and pain. It's particularly hurtful to the parents who attend my Tuesday night support group. Each of these attendees has an adolescent or young adult child with a psychotic disorder. They are mostly pleasant, normal people—no different from you and me, other than that they have crossed the Rubicon into the "mental health system," which is for the most part a non-system of emergency rooms, hospital psychiatric units, day programs, outpatient treatment, psychiatric medications, and taking it one day at a time. They didn't cause their children to experience major mental illness, and they didn't fail to prevent it. This chapter is for people like them.

Why Is Mental Health Care So Hard to Find?

At the time I am writing this, I have worked in the "mental health system" in various capacities for seventeen years, but I can't defend it. My office telephone number forwards to my cell phone, so even when I'm driving my kids to school or shopping for groceries, I get a lot of random calls from people dialing desperately through a long list of numbers. They are usually shocked if I pick up, and they say something like "You're the eleventh person I've called today! My nephew is pacing around and mumbling to himself. Last time he acted like that he tried to kill himself four days later! Can you help him? Just so you know, I'm not rich. No one will answer my messages. The last psychiatrist apparently quit her job four months ago, and we didn't realize until his prescription ran out."

Unfortunately, my answer to most of these people is that I can't help much; my own clinic time and caseload are limited so that I can supervise trainees and conduct research. I do try to listen, offer a reflection or two ("you've been through a lot" or "I can hear how stressful this process has been"), and recommend a person or clinic that might be able to provide what they are seeking. I admit, though, I'm often shaken by these fleeting contacts. In their randomness, they suggest that for everyone who dials my line, there are dozens if not hundreds more with similar circumstances. A father whose son has punched a hole in the wall. A mother whose daughter is hearing voices, but who has been told that the only child psychiatrist who accepts their insurance has no openings for eight weeks. Another mom whose son has tried to hang himself, but who has been sitting alone in an emergency room bay for four days, waiting for a bed on a psychiatric unit to become available so that he can receive treatment for his depression. A twenty-something with bipolar disorder, advocating for herself admirably but confused about who her doctor is and why he's not returning her calls.

I know that my writing risks scaring the uninitiated. I understand the importance of reducing the stigma associated with mental health treatment. Let me assure you that my colleagues are wonderful, smart, altruistic people who are doing their best. We have effective interventions for many conditions, and even scary-sounding treatments like electroconvulsive therapy and antipsychotic medications are delivered with compassion, competence, and precision. Researchers are constantly pursuing innovations to improve the outcomes of both biomedical and psychological therapies. This is very exciting. But sugarcoating the basic situation on the ground, which is that regular people often cannot find acceptable or timely psychiatric treatment, serves no one. The shortage is especially pronounced for kids.

Why has this happened? The prevalence of mental illness, particularly for youth, does appear to be increasing. It's likely that there are novel elements in our environment that are causing harm, though at this point it's not at all clear how much to blame social media or industrial pollutants or excessive use of antibiotics or the increased potency of marijuana products or the fact that parents are conceiving their children at older ages (just to name a few plausible theories). It's also possible that demand for services is higher because caregivers and educators are savvier about identifying potential mental health problems, and the stigma of seeking treatment has diminished. The pandemic also led to increased need for mental health care as kids dealt with sickness, death, disrupted education, isolation, and uncertainty.

I spoke with my colleague Dr. Christine M. Crawford to get a better sense of the barriers she perceives as a practicing child psychiatrist and the associate medical director of the National Alliance on Mental Illness (NAMI). She pointed to a few key issues that create difficulties for families trying to access treatment. The first is that parents don't always recognize signs of mental health problems right away, and sometimes choose to delay care rather than seeking early intervention. But if you have noticed sustained changes in your child's sleep, appetite, or energy; if they are unable to participate in school or social activities; if they are aggressive toward peers or family members or regularly using drugs and alcohol, then it's time to speak with a mental health professional. Other behaviors that shouldn't be ignored or minimized are self-injury, talk of dying, and confusion about what's real and not real (for example, if your child worries that people are plotting against him or interprets odd meaning in everyday events). Second, parents might not know where to go for help. Dr. Crawford suggested starting with pediatricians, who represent the front line in child mental health. Pediatricians can conduct assessments, prescribe psychiatric medications, and refer kids to mental health professionals with whom they work closely.

Third, there is a shortage of qualified pediatric mental health specialists. Training programs for child psychiatrists are long—no different than for other doctors like cardiologists and surgeons. But child psychiatrists usually make less money than other specialists, and they face stigma from a society that questions the validity of psychiatry and accuses providers of overmedicating vulnerable patients. Dr. Crawford points out that popular TV shows and other media tend to glorify surgeons and emergency room doctors as life-saving heroes, while psychiatrists are often portrayed as having ulterior motives, being embroiled in ethical dilemmas, or even having sex with their patients. This doesn't help with recruiting young talent to the field or encouraging people to seek help.

Fourth, in countries where health insurance is ineffective or nonexistent, reimbursements to both patients and providers for mental health care are sometimes laughably inadequate. Many therapists prefer to work as private practitioners rather than in community clinics that accept below-market fees. On the inpatient side, insurance payments to general hospitals do not cover the nursing, equipment, and therapeutic costs of treating patients around the clock for mental health crises; why would a hospital CEO build a brand-new, state-of-the-art psychiatric wing when colonoscopies and joint replacements are so much more lucrative?

If I am describing a situation that is familiar to you, I encourage you to make some noise about it. Hopefully I've made a compelling argument that your child's struggles are not your fault, and you have nothing to be ashamed of. Cancer used to carry such a stigma that doctors often withheld the diagnosis from their patients, and families never uttered the word aloud. Now entire sports leagues wear pink shoes in homage to Breast Cancer Awareness Month. It took brave human beings telling their own stories to create that change in our culture.

Consider sharing your story about the hurdles you faced when trying to get care for your child with your friends, your insurance company, and your representatives at every level of government. Of course, you must consider your kids' privacy; ask them what aspects of their experiences you can reveal. But you shouldn't be afraid to say what you know, which is that your family deserves better.

Hard Talks about Mental Health

Between the stigma of psychiatry and the chaos of the mental health system, many adolescents are reluctant to engage with psychiatric treatment. Additionally, some mental illnesses are characterized by a lack of insight or self-awareness: people truly have no clue that anything about them seems off to others (for more about this topic, read Dr. Xavier Amador's *I Am Not Sick, I Don't Need Help!*). For all these reasons, adolescents may be reluctant to attend appointments, confess their intimate problems to strangers, and generally buy into the idea that therapy or medication will help to solve their problems. Even if your child is under eighteen and thus technically your ward, you cannot compel them to talk openly and vulnerably with a therapist or psychiatrist. If your child is over eighteen, you can't really force them to do anything.

The last issue that Dr. Crawford raised in our conversation as a major barrier to treatment is that parents and other adults don't know how to have productive conversations with kids about flagging mental health issues and finding treatment. "The conversation usually goes like this: *you're failing school; you're not bathing; there's something wrong with you; you need to talk to someone.* It feels confrontational, and kids feel judged. This is not a good place to start," she warns. "If this conversation doesn't go well, it can significantly delay treatment."

I am frequently approached by caregivers who want to know how they can get their relative to accept help, specifically parents who want to convince their adolescent and young adult children to take psychiatric medications. When I describe my five-step method, parents sometimes brush me off at first. "We're in a crisis," they say. "It's not the time to play around. My daughter says she doesn't care if she lives or dies. I need this to happen today."

"What have you already tried?" I ask. Usually, parents have already deployed an array of strategies: reasoning with their child about the need for treatment, providing education about how it will be helpful, reassuring them that it won't be so bad, trying to bribe them with rewards, or threatening consequences if they don't comply. Some parents disclose their own positive experiences with therapy or medication to serve as a role model. Some resort to enrolling their kids in "boot camp" type programs, most of which are unlicensed and some of which have been accused of horrific abuses. At some point, most at least consider an ultimatum: *You can't stay in this house if you don't take your medication.* Of course, most of them would rather not see their mentally ill child sleeping under a bridge, so they have no real intention of following through on this threat.

Parents sometimes find success with these strategies. But if any of them had already worked for the adolescent in question, his or her parents wouldn't be talking to me with a desperate tone in their voices. I don't believe in the concept of "rock bottom" as a precondition for changing difficult patterns of behavior; I believe that people change when they can connect a behavior to their internal motivation and when they feel understood, confident, and in control. That's why, when the stakes are high, I double down on the hard talks method. For parents, this means you should control what you can—lock up (or get rid of) your guns, knives, prescription medicines, and car keys—but even in dire circumstances, you have to negotiate the rest. And if you find yourself in a high-stakes negotiation, you need to bring your most sophisticated conversational skills to the table. Interesting fact: real-life hostage negotiators use an approach similar to motivational interviewing.

Let's consider a few examples in which kids or young adults are facing serious mental health crises. Read on to see how parents can use the hard talks approach to encourage adolescents to connect with treatment. In the first example, a grandmother raises concerns about her grandson's mental health for the first time. In the second, everything has already gone awry, and a father is trying to get back on track with his daughter.

Marcia and Seth

Marcia has always been involved in Seth's life, but it was only last year that he moved in with her full time. Seth's dad has never been around much, but with his grandma, Marcia, living around the corner, he always got plenty of attention. Last year Seth's mom's company offered her an enormous raise to relocate to their Madrid office for three years. It was a hard decision, but she decided to go for it, knowing that this was the opportunity to finally save enough money to buy a house and have financial security when she returned. Seth was twelve at the time and had just been accepted into a prestigious public school with strong connections to post-secondary institutions. He had no interest in leaving his friends and jeopardizing his spot at the school, so Marcia agreed to care for him for the three-year stint.

Everything went smoothly for the first year, but lately Marcia has been noticing some worrying behaviors. Seth is sleeping odd hours, he's withdrawn and moody, and he no longer makes plans to see friends after school and on the weekends. For better or worse, Marcia recognizes the signs of depression, having suffered through some terrible episodes throughout her life. She was about Seth's age and a brand-new immigrant when her own depression started; she doesn't want him to have to go through what she endured. She would like him to talk to a therapist and get some support beyond what she can provide at home. She asks Seth to go for a walk with her in their favorite park with a plan in her head to initiate a hard talk. As they stroll along a quiet trail, she senses that the time is right.

MARCIA: I noticed you haven't invited any friends over to the house in a while. What's behind that?
SETH: I just don't have time. I'm so far behind at school.
MARCIA: You're worried about your grades.

SETH: This school is so crazy. Everyone is so smart, and there's so much pressure around getting into college already. Seventh grade was chill, but now the teachers are assigning a huge amount of reading. It feels impossible.

MARCIA: You can't even take a break to relax with your friends.

SETH: The thing is . . . I take too many breaks. I watch YouTube, I read random stuff on the internet. I procrastinate so much. I feel like an idiot, because I know I'm doing it, but I can't seem to stop. And then I'm behind, way too behind. I wish I could take breaks to see friends. But I'm so dumb, I just waste all my free time. I don't know what's wrong with me. And now my friends have all forgotten about me because I ignored their texts so many times.

MARCIA: Wow, I hear you beating yourself up pretty hard over this. You sound really stressed.

SETH: I am.

MARCIA: That's not a good way to be feeling. Take it from me, I have been there. What will help you with this problem?

SETH: Honestly, nothing. I just need to focus on my work and stop being so dumb.

MARCIA: Can I make a suggestion?

SETH: Sure, what?

MARCIA: I think it would be great for you to talk with that social worker at your school, the one who met with us last year when your mom first left. She seemed very kind and I could tell she cared about you. She said to get in touch with her if you ever need to talk.

SETH: I don't know how she can help me watch less YouTube.

MARCIA: Ha, she probably can't do that. But sometimes talking with the right person who has training in how to deal with pressure and procrastination can make a big difference. What do you think?

SETH: Yeah, okay. I'll try to meet with her.

MARCIA: How will you go about that?

SETH: Oh, I pass by her office every morning. She's always in there. I'll just knock on her door on Monday.

MARCIA: I like that plan. Let me know how it goes. Hey, look—robin's eggs! These must have just hatched.

Marcia did a great job with this hard talk. She picked a calm moment and made a nonjudgmental observation about a change in Seth's behavior. She asked an open-ended question. She did multiple reflections. She resisted her righting reflex, even though it was very painful to hear her grandson saying mean things about himself, and it was so tempting to slide in some organization and time management tips. She asked Seth for his ideas about how to solve the problem. When Seth couldn't think of any, Marcia asked permission before giving advice. She made her suggestion without being pushy. She encouraged Seth—again through questions—to create a specific plan about how to follow through. And then she did not belabor the topic or betray her own longing to control the situation.

One other very successful strategy that Marcia used was to mirror Seth's own description of the problem. Seth described his problem in terms of academic workload and procrastination. Marcia wisely did not label Seth as feeling depressed or use any clinical or medical sounding language. She echoed Seth's own words—pressure, procrastination—as the reasons he might want to talk with a therapist. This is especially important when clinical language might be controversial or introduce stigma. For example, a couple fears that their son is hearing voices and experiencing paranoia; the son maintains that he is stressed out because everyone is spying on him and telling him what to do. An acceptable solution might be to talk with a doctor about the so-called stress. The important part is getting the son to see a doctor as soon as possible, not labeling his problem as psychosis or paranoia.

Gary and Alexis

Twenty-five-year-old Alexis has a complicated relationship with her father, Gary. Gary had sky-high expectations and dreams for his daughter, but Alexis's teenage problems with depression and marijuana evolved into an eventual diagnosis of schizophrenia. After seeing his daughter start and stop taking medications, experience multiple hospitalizations, and get evicted from her apartment, Gary resolved to step up and take control of the situation.

Six months ago he successfully petitioned a court to become Alexis's legal guardian, giving him access to her health records and control of her finances. Finally some leverage, or so he thought. He told her clearly that he would not allow her to spend her disability checks on alcohol or frivolous purchases. He monitored her medical bills for evidence of whether she attended therapy appointments. He accompanied her to her psychiatrist's office and demanded that the doctor give her long-acting medication to address her paranoia, disorganization, and auditory hallucinations. He bought her a gym membership and signed her up for yoga classes. He warned against destructive romantic relationships with damaged, drug-addicted young men, and told her that under no circumstances would he allow drug addicts in his home.

Yet as Gary tightened the reins, Alexis slipped further and further away. Now she never talks to him, other than an occasional text asking for money. Instead of chaotic two a.m. calls, the phone has gone completely silent. And she's still not taking medication or going to therapy. He texts her every day: *You need help, please accept treatment, I'm here, I love you.* No response.

Even a court-approved guardianship yields little actual control if the relationship lacks any sense of partnership. Alexis doesn't like her father's judgments and edicts about her symptoms, friends, and lifestyle. She would rather cut him off and survive on her street smarts than give him any power over her life. So long as she stays out of legal trouble and isn't a threat to herself or others, she has the right to decline treatment for her condition.

This may sound like an extreme situation, but unfortunately, I have seen it play out hundreds of times.

One cruel facet of mental illness is that the symptoms often compromise a person's ability to evaluate their treatment options with any clarity. Depressive hopelessness leads sufferers to feel that there is no point in trying medication or therapy. People in the depths of paranoia don't trust anyone to act in their best interest. And those who have experienced the euphoria of a manic episode often feel that this confident, energetic, lusty version of themselves is their true personality, finally unleashed. Scolding and lecturing by doctors and therapists mostly discourages patients from scheduling additional appointments. Similarly, Gary's disapproval of Alexis and his efforts to control her choices have only diminished his influence in her life. Without a court order for treatment, partnership is the only way forward.

Ready to try a new approach, Gary finds Alexis at one of her favorite hangouts and asks to speak with her alone. She hesitantly agrees.

GARY: It's nice to see you.

ALEXIS: Why are you here?

GARY: I want to talk to you about your appointment with Dr. Hu.

ALEXIS: I don't want to talk to you about that.

GARY: I can tell that it's a private subject for you.

ALEXIS: Yes!

GARY: I understand that. And I promise that I'll just listen, no matter what you say. I'm trying to understand why you don't want to take the medicine that he recommended.

ALEXIS: I don't need it and it makes me gain weight.

GARY: You don't need it.

ALEXIS: Yeah, you and Mom think I'm crazy and I need medication, but I don't.

GARY: You feel like I don't trust your judgment.

ALEXIS: You don't! You think I need a psychiatrist to fix my personality.

GARY: What makes you say that?

ALEXIS: It's true, isn't it?

GARY: I guess I've been pushy about you seeing a psychiatrist because I thought that medication would help you to think more clearly and not hear voices anymore.

ALEXIS: My thinking is fine. And I barely ever hear voices. You make such a big deal out of that.

GARY: So you feel medicine would not be helpful. What do think about therapy?

ALEXIS: I don't know. I liked my last therapist. She was cool.

GARY: What was her name again?

ALEXIS: Like you don't know. You're always lurking, reading about me and talking about me and trying to show the whole world how messed up I am!

GARY: Whoa, whoa. That's an upsetting thought. You think I'm lurking in your medical records.

ALEXIS: You are! That's why I can't talk to her anymore. You ruin everything.

GARY: So if I'm understanding correctly, you stopped meeting with your therapist because you were worried that I would read the notes.

ALEXIS: I wasn't worried—I know what you did!

GARY: I admit, I was checking your medical records. I thought it would be better if I understood what was going on. Maybe I was wrong.

ALEXIS: I knew it! Everyone says I'm paranoid, but you really are spying on me.

GARY: I'm sorry. You're perceptive. It seems like that was a mistake.

ALEXIS: Well, it was.

GARY: What would make you feel comfortable seeing your therapist again? I'm glad to hear you liked her.

ALEXIS: I could never be comfortable with that now that I know you were spying.

GARY: I could never—you, uh—hmm. There's no way to restore trust and privacy.

ALEXIS: No, never.

GARY: I have some ideas. Can I share them?

ALEXIS: I guess.

GARY: I could deactivate my online access to your records. Or maybe we could talk to the therapist together. She might have ideas about how to make sure I can't do that again.

ALEXIS: Hmm. Maybe.

GARY: What do you think?

ALEXIS: I think you're an asshole, to be honest. But yeah, if you delete your access and you tell my therapist that you don't want to read the notes no matter what's in them, then I'll think about meeting her again for therapy.

GARY: Okay, let's do it now. You can watch me delete the account. And do you have the therapist's number in your phone? Let's call her together.

In this hard talk, Gary did not get everything he wanted. Alexis remained adamant (for now) that medications aren't for her. But he didn't give up. When Alexis momentarily slipped into paranoid thinking (*you're always lurking, reading about me and talking about me and trying to show the whole world how messed up I am*), he used a reflection to guess at what she was worried about and show that he was still listening. By listening patiently and choosing not to react to her anger, he learned that his overinvolvement was getting in the way of Alexis's therapy. Once he understood that, he reacted calmly, acknowledged his past behavior, and apologized. He then got back on track with the five steps, asking Alexis if she had any thoughts about how to fix the situation. When she didn't, he asked permission to offer his own ideas, which were acceptable to Alexis. He wasn't able to control her choices, but by using the five steps, he helped her take an important, healthy step toward re-engaging with her therapist.

Seeing your child suffer from mental illness is a terrifying experience. It's not your fault. And you are *not* helpless. Caregivers play a huge role in connecting kids to treatment and supporting their recovery. Don't isolate yourself and further stigmatize your child by treating mental illness like a family secret. Confide in people you can count on to be kind. Don't worry alone.

Hard Talk Highlights

- The best parent in the world cannot prevent illnesses like depression, bipolar disorder, schizophrenia, eating disorders, or anxiety in their child.

- Between the stigma of psychiatry and the chaos of the mental health system, many adolescents are reluctant to engage with psychiatric treatment.

- People don't need to hit rock bottom before changing difficult patterns of behavior; people change when they can connect a behavior to their internal motivation, and when they feel understood, confident, and in control.

- Seeing your child suffer from mental illness is a terrifying experience. It's not your fault. And you are *not* helpless. Caregivers play a huge role in connecting kids to treatment and supporting their recovery.

CHAPTER 10
HOW TO PRACTICE HARD TALKS

Well, here we are. You've read the book and you want to try the hard talks method at home. But you want some practice before you're ready for prime time (prime time, of course, being a white-knuckle conversation with your adolescent about safe sex or alcohol: fun!).

You don't have to wait until a hard talk is unavoidable to try out reflections, questions, and asking permission before giving advice. As I've described throughout this book, these are skills that can fit into everyday interactions to improve communication and listening. When I teach the School of Hard Talks to groups of parents, we play a game during the final hour. I call it the You Can Do This game. I read off typical adolescent one-liners in a rapid-fire style, and parents race to come up with motivational interviewing-consistent responses (a reflection, question, or affirmation) as if they're on a game show. Turn the page for some examples:

I don't know what to wear.	<li>What will you be doing?</li><li>Looking good for this event is important to you.</li>
I got an A in history!	<li>You sound so proud!</li><li>Hooray! How do you want to celebrate?</li><li>You've worked hard for that!</li>
I hate the new basketball coach.	<li>I can tell you're really frustrated.</li><li>Tell me more.</li>
I want a tattoo.	<li>What's behind that?</li><li>What is the time frame for that decision?</li><li>What do you see as the pros and cons?</li>

It's a silly game, but it helps parents to identify the many, many opportunities they will have to use their new skills. And if they feel like they blew an opportunity by letting their righting reflex get the better of them or losing their temper, the game reminds them that another chance is always around the corner.

Some parents like to first try their new skills in the "shallow end"—that is, when discussing completely noncontroversial topics. One mom told me that she was driving with her daughter and practiced curious questions by offering to let her daughter choose some songs for them to listen to. She asked open-ended questions about the songs her daughter chose: *What band is this? What is this song is about? What do you like about it?*

The mom told me this was the longest, most rewarding conversation they'd had in years. After this conversation, she felt more confident that she could also use the skills to talk to her son about more difficult topics, such as his substance use and money management.

Trying out these skills in different settings and in different relationships is another way to practice. You can practice on a friend, coworker, or romantic partner. Once you start to look for opportunities to use these skills, you will find many. Colleague complaining about a difficult client? *What a mess! What are you gonna do?* Spouse describing the latest extended family drama? *Are you looking for advice, or should I just focus on listening?* Friend venting about her ex? *So he totally ignored your call. Wow!*

Parents often tell me stories of how they found themselves successfully deploying motivational interviewing in unexpected situations. One woman, who works as a foreign language interpreter, told me that she was interpreting a conversation between an attorney and his agitated client. When the attorney offered a series of reflections, she got to try the skill for herself by translating the statements to the client. She experienced firsthand how the attorney's reflections de-escalated the client's emotion and paved the way for a more productive conversation. Another mom relayed that she used questions and reflections in a tense customer service situation and wound up receiving a massive discount that was supposedly not available moments before.

These are all examples of how you can practice skills with an oblivious audience. If you have a willing practice partner, then you can do what we call a real play. Real play is a fantastic way to learn and practice motivational interviewing. To do a real play, one person shares a real-life dilemma—a decision they are struggling to make or a change they've been putting off: *I want to exercise more. I can't decide whether it's time get a new car. Should we spend the holidays at home or with my in-laws?* The other person then uses the five-step guide from Chapter 7 to help resolve the dilemma. At any point the person whose dilemma is being discussed can pause the conversation to provide feedback. Feedback might sound like this: *I feel like you're pushing me into a decision. Try asking more questions. I'm feeling a little judged. I know you've been through something similar, but can we focus on my situation right now?* Feedback can also be positive: *What a great question! I've never thought about it that way. Thank you for pointing that out. It's so nice to talk to someone who really listens.* In this way, both people get to learn in real time what works and how to best use the skills.

So if you're feeling brave, grab a friend and try it. Be gentle with one another. I'm rooting for you.

Hard Talk Highlights

- You don't have to wait until a hard talk is unavoidable to try out reflections, questions, and asking permission before giving advice.

- Some parents like to first try out their new skills while discussing completely noncontroversial topics.

- You can also practice the method with a friend or partner and ask for feedback.

ACKNOWLEDGMENTS

I would like to thank my amazing team and the collaborators who helped develop and test the School of Hard Talks and Motivational Interviewing for Loved Ones content. Heather Thibeau, thank you for your positivity, dedication, and competence in all things. Aliyah Simone Sanders, Beshaun Davis, Alicia Fenley, Bediha Ipekci, and Jada Gibbs, you are the dream team. You've made work fun or at least deeply meaningful every day. Collectively and individually, you rise above every challenge, COVID-related and otherwise. Thank you. Kelly English, thank you for being the first person to get excited about this idea and assembling an inclusive brain trust to kick-start it. Theresa McIntyre, thank you for your big heart, fantastic ideas, and advocacy on behalf of Boston families. Thank you Sharyn Rosart, Sasquatch Books, and Spruce Books for the opportunity to share the School of Hard Talks with parents far and wide.

I'd also like to thank a few of my many generous mentors, starting with Matcheri "Kesh" Keshavan, who has always treated my success as inevitable while offering excellent and practical advice. I wish I could thank Larry Seidman, who brought me to Boston and taught me science and diplomacy in equal measure. Thank you Jason Schiffman, who helped me understand

and develop my talents. Thank you Jessica Feldman, who got me running in the right direction nearly twenty years ago, and Jennifer Stone, who showed me how to be a therapist.

Shout-out to the Boston Medical Center WRAP team, especially Hannah Brown. I'm so proud to be part of this hardworking and excellent crew. Thank you to Christine Crawford and Dave Henderson for sharing your insights, and to Christina Borba, whose favorite words are *cool, great,* and *go for it!*

I can't believe my good fortune when I wake up every day with Andy Rosen and the two sweet, passionate, wickedly smart little people who share our home. Thank you for being you, a brilliant confidant, humorist, father, chef, hype-man, citizen, and writer. I was also blessed to grow up in a great family, a loving and boisterous extended family, and idyllic neighborhood. Thank you to my parents for their constancy, encouragement, and support. Thank you to the people, places, and institutions of my own adolescence in Pittsburgh's East End. Is it too much to add that I also married into a terrific clan? Well, it's the truth. I can't account for my blessings. I hope you all recognize the best bits of yourselves in this book.

I would like to acknowledge the National Institute of Mental Health, which funded my research through a mentored career development grant, K23MH118373. Finally, my sincerest thanks and respect to the families who participated in my research studies, and to all who generously share their tissues, images, stories, and time with researchers for the betterment of humankind.

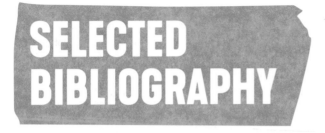

SELECTED BIBLIOGRAPHY

CHAPTER 1

Harris, Judith Rich. *The Nurture Assumption: Why Children Turn Out the Way They Do*. New York: Simon & Schuster, 2011.

Steinberg, Laurence. *Age of Opportunity: Lessons from the New Science of Adolescence*. Boston: Houghton Mifflin Harcourt, 2014.

UNICEF. "Ensuring Mental Health and Well-being in an Adolescent's Formative Years Can Foster a Better Transition from Childhood to Adulthood." Mental Health (October 2021). https://data.unicef.org/topic/child-health/mental-health.

Substance Abuse and Mental Health Services Administration. "Key Substance Use and Mental Health Indicators in the United States: Results from the 2019 National Survey on Drug Use and Health." (September 2020). www.samhsa.gov/data/sites/default/files/reports/rpt29393/2019NSDUHFFRPDFWHTML/2019NSDUHFFR1PDFW090120.pdf.

Mental Health Foundation. "Teenagers' Mental Health under Severe Pressure as Pandemic Continues: New Research." (2021). www.mentalhealth.org.uk/news/teenagers-mental-health-pandemic.

Mott Poll Report. "How the Pandemic Has Impacted Teen Mental Health." (March 2021). www.mottpoll.org/reports/how-pandemic-has-impacted-teen-mental-health.

Dennon, Anne. "Over Nine in Ten College Students Report Mental Health Impacts from COVID-19." (April 2021). www.bestcolleges.com/research/college-mental-health-impacts-from-covid-19.

Kline, Emily R. et al. "Motivational Interviewing for Loved Ones in Early Psychosis: Development and Pilot Feasibility Trial of a Brief Psychoeducational Intervention for Caregivers." *Frontiers in Psychiatry* 12 (April 2021): 421.

Kline, Emily R. et al. "The School of Hard Talks: A Telehealth Parent Training Group for Caregivers of Adolescents and Young Adults." *Early Intervention in Psychiatry* (June 2022).

Butzlaff, Ronald L., and Jill M. Hooley. "Expressed Emotion and Psychiatric Relapse: A Meta-Analysis." *Archives of General Psychiatry* 55, no. 6 (1998): 547–52.

Peris, Tara S., and David J. Miklowitz. "Parental Expressed Emotion and Youth Psychopathology: New Directions for an Old Construct. *Child Psychiatry & Human Development* 46, no. 6 (2015): 863–73.

Wiedemann, Georg et al. "The Family Questionnaire: Development and Validation of a New Self-report Scale for Assessing Expressed Emotion. *Psychiatry Research* 109, no. 3 (2002): 265–79.

Robinson, Raz. "More Than Half of Parents Admit They Struggle to Hold a Conversation with Their Kids." (2018). www.fatherly.com/news /survey-half-parents-struggle-hold-conversation-with-kids.

CHAPTER 2

Baumrind, Diana. "Child Care Practices Anteceding Three Patterns of Preschool Behavior." *Genetic Psychology Monographs* 75, no. 1 (1967): 43–88.

Baumrind, Diana. "The Influence of Parenting Style on Adolescent Competence and Substance Use." *Journal of Early Adolescence* 11, no. 1 (1991): 56–95.

Arnett, Jeffrey Jensen, and Jennifer Lynn Tanner, eds. *Emerging Adults in America: Coming of Age in the Twenty-First Century.* Washington, DC: American Psychological Association Press, 2005.

Miller, William R., and Stephen Rollnick. *Motivational Interviewing: Helping People Change*. New York: Guilford Press, 2012.

Lundahl, Brad et al. "Motivational Interviewing in Medical Care Settings: A Systematic Review and Meta-analysis of Randomized Controlled Trials." *Patient Education and Counseling* 93, no, 2 (2013): 157–68.

DiClemente, Carlo C. et al. "Motivational Interviewing, Enhancement, and Brief Interventions over the Last Decade: A Review of Reviews of Efficacy and Effectiveness." *Psychology of Addictive Behaviors* 31, no. 8 (2017): 862.

Rogers, Carl R. *On Becoming a Person: A Therapist's View of Psychotherapy*. Boston: Houghton Mifflin. 1995.

CHAPTER 3

Stone, Elizabeth. *A Boy I Once Knew*. New York: Workman Publishing. 2002.

CHAPTER 5

Suzuki, Shunryu. *Zen Mind, Beginner's Mind*. Boulder: Shambhala Publications, 2011.

Heschel, Abraham Joshua. *God in Search of Man: A Philosophy of Judaism*. New York: Farrar, Strauss and Giroux, 1955.

CHAPTER 6

Personal interview with Dr. David Henderson, April 1, 2022.

Gershoff, Elizabeth T. et al. "Parent Discipline Practices in an International Sample: Associations with Child Behaviors and Moderation by Perceived Normativeness." *Child Development* 81, no. 2 (2010): 487–502.

Kohn, Alfie. *Punished by Rewards: The Trouble with Gold Stars, Incentive Plans, A's, Praise, and Other Bribes*. Boston: Houghton Mifflin, 2018.

CHAPTER 8

Gottman, John M., and Robert W. Levenson. "What Predicts Change in Marital Interaction Over Time? A Study of Alternative Models." *Family Process* 38, no. 2 (1999): 143–58.

Brown, Brené. "Shame Resilience Theory: A Grounded Theory Study on Women and Shame." *Families in Society* 87, no. 1 (2006): 43–52.

CHAPTER 9

Personal interview with Dr. Christine M. Crawford, March 15, 2022.

National Academy of Sciences. "Can Mental and Emotional Disorders Be Prevented?" Health (2020). www.thesciencebehindit.org/can-mental-and-emotional-disorders-be-prevented.

Association for Behavioral Healthcare. "Outpatient Mental Health Access and Workforce Crisis Issue Brief." (February 2022). www.abhmass.org/images/resources/ABH_Outpatient MHAccessWorkforce/Outpatient_survey_issue_brief_FINAL.pdf.

Amador, Xavier. *I'm Not Sick, I Don't Need Help!* Utah: Vida Press, 2007.

Rosen, Kenneth R. *Troubled: The Failed Promise of America's Behavioral Treatment Programs*. New York: Little a, 2021.

Barker, Eric. "Six Hostage Negotiation Techniques That Will Get You What You Want." *Time* (2014). www.time.com/38796/6-hostage-negotiation-techniques-that-will-get-you-what-you-want.

RECOMMENDED RESOURCES

ONLINE

The School of Hard Talks Online: https://handholdma.org/what-can
-i-do/the-school-of-hard-talks-online-lessons-from-motivational
-interviewing-for-everyday-families

The National Alliance on Mental Illness: www.nami.org

PRINT

Duckworth, Ken. *You Are Not Alone: The NAMI Guide to Mental Illness and Recovery.* New York: Zando, 2022.

ANYTIME CRISIS SUPPORT

United States: **988** is the new National Suicide Prevention Lifeline. Just like 911, you can dial 988 anytime from anywhere in the country to be connected to a trained crisis intervention specialist.

Canada: The Canada Suicide Prevention Service has 24/7 support available at **1-833-456-4566**.

United Kingdom: Text SHOUT to **85258** anytime from anywhere in the United Kingdom to connect to a trained crisis volunteer.

Australia: Call **13-11-14** or text **0477-13-11-14** anytime to connect to a trained volunteer.

New Zealand: Call or text **1737** any time for counseling or support.

An online search for "crisis hotline" will lead you to helpful resources wherever you are.

INDEX

ABOUT THE AUTHOR

Emily Kline, PhD, is a clinical psychologist and writer in Boston. She has held faculty positions in psychiatry at Boston University School of Medicine and Harvard Medical School. She completed her bachelor's degree at Haverford College, her graduate training at the University of Maryland, Baltimore County, and her clinical and postdoctoral fellowships at Harvard Medical School. She lives with her husband and children who graciously beta-test her experiments in family communication, and a dog who can't be reasoned with at all.